INDIA

VS

UK

The Story of an
Unprecedented Diplomatic Win

INDIA
VS
UK

Syed Akbaruddin

HarperCollins *Publishers* India

First published in India in 2021 by
HarperCollins *Publishers*
A-75, Sector 57, Noida, Uttar Pradesh 201301, India
www.harpercollins.co.in

2 4 6 8 10 9 7 5 3 1

P-ISBN: 978-93-5489-203-5
E-ISBN: 978-93-5489-093-2

Typeset in 11/15.2 Berling LT Std at
Manipal Technologies Limited, Manipal

Printed and bound at
Replika Press Pvt. Ltd.

Dedicated
to
India's diplomatic fraternity

Contents

Prologue
Starting Off on the Wrong Foot

IN SITUATIONS OF global flux, changes happen. Shifts occur although they are not always planned and plotted for. At times, fault lines long in the making come to the fore due to unforeseen circumstances. In multilateral diplomacy, such changes are rare but not unknown. They have a bearing that is little understood when they occur. Their impact tends to unveil itself only over a protracted period of time. Nevertheless, a record of events is always useful to make sense of the changes and place them in proper perspective.

Since Independence, India's foreign policy orientation has always included a strong commitment to multilateralism. In fact, being present at the inception of the United Nations (UN) as a founding member, as it was in the League of Nations too even prior to Independence, makes for our historical uniqueness in this key multilateral forum. It is a truism that since then Indian diplomacy has excelled in several aspects of multilateral diplomacy. This has manifested in myriad ways. Setting pioneering agendas, promoting policy options beneficial for developing states, bridge-building in complex treaty negotiations, promoting the global observance of common civilizational values, the rendering of dedicated services by very many Indians in international civil service, and the stellar contributions of Indian military personnel on UN peacekeeping missions are a few of the many facets of India's role at the UN that can be listed and buttressed with numerous examples.

Independent India, however, started off its journey on the wrong foot in one crucial aspect of multilateral diplomacy— winning in major elections.[1] It was around midday of 30 September 1947. The General Assembly was having its second session, the first after India's Independence. The UN did not yet have its permanent premises along the East River in mid-town Manhattan. The meeting was being held in New York City at Flushing Meadows, Corona Park, in the suburb of Queens. The venue was where the Queens Museum's sky-lit gallery would come to be established later. Presiding over the session was the Brazilian politician and diplomat Oswaldo Aranha. On the agenda was the election of three non-permanent members of the Security Council to replace Australia, Brazil and Poland, whose terms would end on 31 December 1947. In the fray were Argentina, Canada, Czechoslovakia, the Ukrainian Soviet Socialist Republic, Uruguay and newly independent India. Those elected would join the Security Council on 1 January 1948. The UN had fifty-seven members, including Pakistan, which had been admitted as the fifty-sixth member earlier in the day, consequent to a vote on account of Afghanistan's objection.[2] The required two-third majority for election as a non-permanent member meant that thirty-eight votes would have to be won out of the fifty-seven valid votes. Argentina and Canada both were elected in the first round of voting with forty-one votes each.[3] The Ukrainian Soviet Socialist Republic with thirty-three votes and India with twenty-nine were placed third and fourth respectively and were required to have a direct contest to decide who would fill the third seat.[4]

It took more than forty days and a dozen votes for the outcome to be decided. India withdrew as the Ukrainian Soviet Socialist Republic consistently out-polled it in every vote. Around midday of 13 November 1947, the Ukrainian Soviet Socialist Republic was declared elected, polling thirty-five out of thirty-seven valid votes, two invalid ballots and fifteen abstentions. The required majority threshold was twenty-six votes.[5]

This first defeat of independent India in a significant multilateral election in the UN General Assembly meant that India's engagement with the Security Council was not about to begin as a decision-maker on peace and security, but as a plaintiff. It was on 6 January 1948 that the Security Council first considered the India–Pakistan question, an item that remains on the agenda more than seventy years later.[6]

Elections at the UN, almost always, are an inter-state contest. Even when they are formally intended to choose independent individuals, the state from which the individual hails is inevitably the most significant factor. The UN platform is one of inter-state contestation. States play a pivotal role in every election at the UN—not only as voters but also as the principal backers and supporters of the candidates nominated by them or by others on their behalf. Consequently, success or the lack of it in any multilateral election is primarily on account of the efforts of states, rather than individuals.

No election is as 'political' and hotly contested as the one for independent judges of the International Court of Justice (ICJ). A year after India's Independence, in 1948, the eminent jurist Dr B.N. Rau was a candidate to a seat of the ICJ. The complicated electoral process made the ICJ elections the most complex in the entire UN system. The election went into multiple rounds in both the bodies (General Assembly and Security Council), which voted simultaneously and independently to elect five judges. Alas, India's nominee fell short when the final results were announced.[7]

Since then, India has contested successfully in hundreds of UN elections. But then, as they say, there are 'Elections' and then there are other 'elections'. India has contested ten more elections to the Security Council since, winning eight of them. These were elections in the UN sense of the term—in that they required balloting. However, many were contests without competition. Seven times, India went into the Security Council elections on a 'clean slate'.[8] There was no competitor from the group we were contesting. In many cases, we had the 'endorsement' of the group. This made the ballot less of a stress test, as victory was ensured without a contest.

Only once, for the term of 1967-68, did we win a 'competitive' election to the Security Council against Syria in one round.[9] The rest of the times when we did not have a clean slate at the regional level, we lost. In 1975, contesting against Pakistan in an election which went through multiple rounds, we withdrew—paving the way for Pakistan to join the Council in 1976-77.[10] Then in 1996, we suffered a huge single-round loss to Japan.[11]

Candidates from India also contested many more times for a seat at the ICJ following the loss in 1948. Yet, never had a first effort by an Indian candidate for a full term to the ICJ resulted in victory until Judge Dalveer Bhandari won a full nine-year term in a historic election in 2017.

Before this, two other candidates from India had contested and won three full nine-year terms. Both were, however, candidates who had contested earlier and lost, before they won their first full term. They won when they contested at the next election, having made their candidature plans known years in advance. Dr B.N. Rau, having lost in 1948, contested again in 1951, when he was the Indian Permanent Representative to the UN. He won in the first round of balloting.[12] Similarly, Dr Nagendra Singh, having lost in 1969, contested again in 1972, when he was India's Chief Election Commissioner. He won after a single round in the General Assembly[13] and resigned as the Chief Election Commissioner to take his seat at the ICJ in 1973. In 1981, after having completed his full nine-year term, he sought re-election as a sitting judge and easily won again in two quick rounds of balloting in the course of the same meeting.[14]

The rest of the elections that we contested and won to the ICJ were only for the remainder of the unfinished terms of incumbents who either died or resigned.[15] Fundamentally, these are different types of elections and similar to bye-elections.

Major elections at the UN do not usually engender excitement in the outside world. Within the UN system, they are often a useful barometer of the standing of an individual member state at a particular juncture and the mood of other UN members. They bring together all elements of a state's acumen in multilateral diplomacy as well as a state's ability to leverage the intensity of bilateral ties to its advantage on the global platform. They are also a useful way of understanding the ground realities that diplomats are required to navigate in fulfilling foreign policy objectives.

Against this background, India's success in the titanic election tussle of 2017, upending all past precedents, is a good case study to understand the changing contours of India's recent approach to global fora. How and why did India decide to contest this election? What was the decision-making process? What were the stakes involved? How did this election metamorphose into one which upturned conventions and ended with a paradigm shift never witnessed before in the history of UN elections? What were the key factors in India's success? Who helped and what were the hindrances? What was the difference in India's approach so that it could avoid becoming, to use a sporting term, a 'choker'? What were the lessons learnt? What does it augur for India's future role at the UN and beyond?

Foreign policy is about grand strategy as well as about getting the nuts and bolts of diplomacy right. This is all the more so amidst the tumult that the global order is currently confronting. While high-profile events gather attention, unpublicized shifts in working methods that take place below the formal level also are important ingredients of quiet changes. Cooperating, coordinating, agreeing and implementing mutually agreed goals with a wide and diverse array of partners may not catch attention but are as important as visualizing, designing, strategizing and planning policies with key global players. Even as, understandably, the focus is on the big-ticket items, little-noticed subterranean changes in the broader framework of continuity in India's recent diplomatic experience are also making a difference. These changes are, as yet, an evolving narrative that has still to be told. This book is a contribution towards telling that story.

Unlike a big-picture narration, a description of subterranean changes is about explaining a maze. Since any world-wide effort depends on getting numerous moving parts right, it isn't possible to depict all the complex manoeuvres that go into the making of a global foreign policy success, irrespective of the vantage point of a narrator. The choice is between telling a partial story and not telling any story at all. Telling stories about institutions and practices is also about shoring up their foundations and building on their edifices. If stories are not told about the many facets that help institutions evolve, then nuggets tend to be lost and successful practices that need to be institutionalized tend to atrophy. This reconstruction has ventured to narrate developments as they evolved, as best as one can, even while acknowledging that no single actor can see all or tell all. It has drawn upon a long-time habit of regular and copious dairy notings kept over a period of four years. To ensure that the flavour of situations as they happened is not lost, the jottings are largely reproduced in the contemporaneous style that they were written in. They have, however, been supplemented by adding from memory encounters that have left a lasting impression and by drawing substantive details of formal outcomes from UN official records.

Diplomacy is often associated with abstract notions such as national interests, sovereignty, international law, justice, order, balance of power, hard power and soft power. However, individuals do play a significant role in translating these concepts into action. In the practice of foreign policy, people matter. This is a recollection of the roles that various people played in fulfilling a foreign policy objective. While some key actors are widely known, many are little known. Nevertheless, they played crucial roles. They may be the proverbial cogs which have kept the machinery of Indian diplomacy running. Their contributions are rarely acknowledged. Yet, without them there would have been no diplomatic success in the form that it was achieved. The result was 'sui generis' or one of its kind. It had not happened ever before in the annals of the UN. It will be difficult for any country to replicate it in the future too. This is an account of that saga.

Finally, in recounting the events related to this story of an unprecedented Indian diplomatic success, I unabashedly plead guilty to entirely following Graham Greene's memorable dictum from *The End of the Affair*, that 'a story has no beginning or end: arbitrarily one chooses that moment of experience from which to look back or from which to look ahead'.

1

It Began with a Whisper

Friday, 19 February 2016
New York

IT IS MORE than a month since I assumed charge on 5 January 2016 as India's Permanent Representative to the UN in New York. Yet, every day, as I enter the premises of the Indian Mission to the UN, crossing the huge brass doors that form our 'Golden Gate' and walk through the hallway on the ground floor where the photos of all Indian Permanent Representatives presenting their credentials are on display, I feel overawed by where I have landed.

It is not as if either New York or the UN is new to me. In the mid-1990s, I served for three years as First Secretary here, sandwiched between stints at the Ministry of External Affairs in New Delhi and the High Commission of India in Islamabad. A decade later too, as an international civil servant with the International Atomic Energy Agency (IAEA) in Vienna, I travelled to the UN headquarters regularly. As Special Assistant to the Director General of the IAEA, I had worked on UN-related policy issues, including the Iranian nuclear dossier for five years. Subsequently, as the Official Spokesperson of the Ministry of External Affairs, I had accompanied several external affairs ministers and two prime ministers annually as part of the Indian delegation to the high-level segment of the General Assembly in September.

However, no amount of engagement with the substance of multilateral issues can help overcome the inadequacy one feels when assuming the responsibility of representing more than a billion people on the global stage every day. No length of multilateral experience is enough to help one slide into this role. Many of my illustrious predecessors had stellar records of public service. For example, Dr B.N. Rau, the first Permanent Representative, had served as the Constitutional Adviser to India's Constituent Assembly. Ambassador Brajesh Mishra had, after retirement, gone on to become India's first National Security Adviser and was also Principal Secretary to Prime Minister Atal Bihari Vajpayee, a dual role which no one else has been entrusted with. Ambassador Hamid Ansari had risen to become the Vice President of India. Also, it is widely expected that a more recent predecessor, Ambassador Hardeep Singh Puri, who is still engaged with a New York-based think tank, will soon get an important role in the Indian government. Following in the steps of such stalwarts is an overwhelming experience.

Whenever I meet a colleague from another country while going through the time-consuming but necessary process of 'courtesy calls', I feel humbled by what they share of their past experiences with former Indian diplomats. To me, such meetings are more than a mere courtesy. They are opportunities for sharing information that one may not otherwise come across easily. They are occasions when newcomers not only get to know old-timers but can seek advice and guidance, exchange anecdotes, connect with old friends and make new ones. They are essential diplomatic rites of passage. I, therefore, am keen to have such meetings with as many of the 190 or so ambassadors at the UN as I can, even as I realize that I may not be able to call on all. Diplomats are, after all, modern-day nomads who keep moving from one place to another. Some are likely to move on to new destinations even before our meetings materialize. Nevertheless, the goal is to meet all.

This afternoon, the unfathomable value of such courtesy meetings is on full display. It relates to a discovery that catches me completely off-guard. It was not going through an analytical report or the pursuit of thoughtfully planned instructions that led to this discovery. I fortuitously stumble on to it, through that most essential but underrated of diplomatic tools—the whisper.

The quiet confines of the Indonesian Lounge is a favourite of many diplomats who like to have a quick chat without attracting the notice of others. The cosy corner is so named as the Government of Indonesia had initially gifted artefacts and furniture placed in this part of the UN building. While others have since been forthcoming with contributions that embellished the space, the name has stuck. In the course of a courtesy meeting in this frequently used location with a French-speaking colleague from West Africa, I am confronted with a question for which I am entirely unprepared.

'When are you beginning your campaign for the International Court of Justice?' he pointedly asks in the midst of our conversation about Indian diplomats with whom he has worked during his various stints at the UN, spread over nearly four decades.

Seeing me nonplussed, he leans across the banquette on which he is seated. I am momentarily distracted. My eyes turn towards the stunning 'Kishwah', the black brocade cloth with gold embroidered calligraphy that covers the most sacred shrine of Islam, the Ka'bah in Makkah. It is usually changed annually, cut into pieces and distributed as a relic. It is a gift from the Kingdom of Saudi Arabia to the UN and now on display in full splendour in the lounge. Realizing that he has lost me, he draws me close to him and, after glancing towards the adjacent General Assembly Hall, as if to make sure that there is no one else watching or listening, he whispers, 'Don't leave it for too long. Watch out, Dr Nawaf Salam has been pressing ahead for some time.'

The elections to the ICJ are scheduled to be held in November 2017. There are more than twenty months to go. Neither the immersive briefing notes that I have gone through in Delhi, as preparation for my assignment, nor the detailed position papers provided on my arrival in New York by the talented team of diplomats at the Permanent Mission of India have mentioned the subject. Also, no one I met in Delhi or New York alluded to this as an issue of consequence. Simply put, the ICJ election is not on anyone's radar in our diplomatic establishment. Yet, here is a well-informed diplomat, from a country that we do not even have a resident diplomatic presence in, pointing me towards a nugget of information that I have no knowledge about.

With my antennae raised, I return to the Indian Mission as the grey winter evening is being enveloped by darkness. As is my usual practice, I ask Ambassador Tanmaya Lal, the erudite Deputy Permanent Representative, to meet me so that we can discuss this discovery. Ambassador Lal, or Tanmaya as he is referred to by all in the Indian Foreign Service community, is an engineer by training, with a master's degree in science. Scientific rigour is always reflected in his thinking and writing.

He opted to join the Permanent Mission less than a month ago, giving up the opportunity to serve as his own boss in most other Indian diplomatic outposts.

'I want you to research the background and prepare a detailed evaluation about the ICJ election process and our interest in it,' I request Tanmaya after narrating the broad contours of my conversation with the extraordinarily well-disposed African counterpart.

'I need some time before I get back to you,' is Tanmaya's understandably cautious response. He too has been taken by surprise, even though he had assiduously prepared himself in New Delhi before joining in New York. Both of us need time to chew this over before we can proceed to lay out the issues for decision-making systematically.

Tuesday, 1 March – Thursday, 31 March 2016
New York

Delving into our repository of record with the help of a young election officer, First Secretary Noor Rahman Sheikh, Tanmaya comes up with a detailed and incisive analysis that provides the background and lays out the present situation that we face.

In 2012, Judge Dalveer Bhandari,[1] a former judge of India's Supreme Court, replaced Judge Awn Shawkat Al-Khasawneh[2] of Jordan, who had resigned in 2011, three years into his second term. It was a not-so-well-kept secret that when he was contesting for a second term in 2008, Judge Al-Khasawneh, rather than face an Indian challenge, had reached an understanding that at a certain stage in his second term he would yield his place, opening an early opportunity for a successor. As fate would have it, Judge Al-Khasawneh was appointed Prime Minister of Jordan, so he resigned from the ICJ.[3]

Mid-term elections to fill vacancies to the ICJ are only for the incomplete terms of the judges who leave the bench. In this case, it was for less than six of the nine-year term of an ICJ judge. India was serving as a non-permanent member of the Security Council in 2011-12. It was also well understood that an Indian candidate for the ICJ had been contemplated for long and dated back at least to the elections in 2008. In the campaign spearheaded by the redoubtable Ambassador Hardeep Puri, Indian nominee Judge Bhandari easily prevailed in a single round on 27 April 2012 against his only opponent, Judge Florentino Feliciano of the Philippines.[4]

Now, in early 2016, we need to decide if we are willing to contest for a seat on the ICJ again. On the other hand, Dr Nawaf Salam—Nawaf, as he is popularly known in the diplomatic fraternity at the UN—is an astute diplomat. He has built personal equities during the decade-long stay as the Ambassador of Lebanon to the UN. Nawaf, according to the West African colleague, is diligently pursuing a cherished personal goal by assiduously converting the verbal IOUs ('I Owe You') to concrete support for his candidature for the ICJ.

The case that Nawaf is making is simple. In 2012, Lebanon had fielded a candidate for the ICJ when India fielded Judge Bhandari to replace Judge Al-Khasawneh of Jordan. Lebanon had withdrawn even though the seat was held by an Arab judge. The hope was that, following the end of the remaining six-year period, Judge Bhandari would not contest again in 2017 as the rotation of incumbents of such seats helps everyone get an opportunity. Unknown to our diplomatic establishment,

Nawaf's efforts to replace India's Judge Bhandari at the ICJ have been gathering steam for quite some time.

Tanmaya's conclusion, prepared after a couple of weeks of studying the available material and based on subsequent soundings by other diplomats, is that the election cycle of November 2016–November 2017 will be a rare period for us. Three elections will be held for key UN legal bodies— the International Law Commission (ILC),[5] the International Tribunal for the Law of the Seas (ITLOS)[6] and the International Court of Justice (ICJ).[7] India has incumbents on each of these bodies. Given that the elections to these institutions are usually held at different intervals, over a nine-year period we have got our nationals elected to each of them. We now need to decide if we are willing to contest all the three in the space of a year. If so, we will be the only country to do so. We should choose with care and caution, decide early and begin the pursuit of our chosen objectives forthwith.

⸺◦◦◦⸺

Friday, 1 April – Saturday, 31 December 2016
New York and New Delhi

When difficult choices are posed, uncertainty about receiving responses is not unusual. It is so in this instance too. Months of silence have followed the first dispatch sent by Noor Rahman Sheikh from New York in March 2016. In accordance with usual practice, Tanmaya has followed up our initial message. Three months later, in June 2016, he is still awaiting a response. More silence. It is not yet a case of 'no'. The first 'no' is yet to be received. For the present, we remain uncertain.

In between this prolonged silence, in April 2016, we receive directions to field Dr Aniruddha Rajput as the candidate for the ILC election to be held in November 2016. The ILC is a subsidiary organ of the General Assembly. It has a mandate to assist in the codification and progressive development of international law. It is composed of thirty-four members who serve in their individual capacities for a five-year term.[8] The ILC is also considered a staging post to a subsequent international judicial position. By some accounts, seven of the current ICJ judges have served as ILC members, and thirty-six ILC members have served as judges of the ICJ.[9]

India is usually represented on the ILC by a government functionary. However, in a departure from past practice, a bright young lawyer with no previous international exposure has been chosen. The decision does not go down well with the cadre of the Legal and Treaties Division of the Ministry of External Affairs, which treats this seat as its preserve. Some from among them ally with those who want to criticize the choice on the grounds that many qualified public international law experts, from the government and academic fraternities, have been overlooked in favour of a young sympathizer of the ruling dispensation.[10] The brouhaha makes us at the Permanent Mission determined to get Dr Rajput elected to the ILC in November 2016 with a wide margin.

Even as we are pursuing Dr Rajput's election, we keep seeking answers to the question of whether India will also contest the ICJ election. Nawaf formally announces his candidature in April 2016. All the other sitting judges whose terms are ending—Brazil's Judge Antônio Augusto Cançado Trindade,[11] France's Judge Ronny Abraham,[12] Somalia's Judge Abdulqawi Ahmed Yusuf[13] and the UK's Judge Christopher

Greenwood[14]—are pursuing re-election. Five candidates are already eyeing the five seats available.

In August 2016, amidst Dr Rajput's election campaign comes another decision. Dr Neeru Chadha, who had headed our Legal and Treaties Division prior to her retirement in 2015 and whose candidature for the ILC had been overlooked earlier, is to be India's candidate for the ITLOS in June 2017. A knowledgeable lawyer who has served India's cause on many tribunals and cases, she is a popular choice. Her nomination reinforces our belief that the ICJ is not a priority. Contesting two major legal elections in a span of six months is already a tall order, so we think that three elections in a year is a non-starter.

Brazil, which had previously put in its candidature for both the ICJ and the ITLOS, is not going to pursue candidacy for the ITLOS, deciding instead to focus on the ICJ. Lebanon, which submitted its candidature for both elections, is making no effort to canvass for its ITLOS candidate, acknowledging defeat well in advance. All others, including France, Germany, the Netherlands, the Republic of Korea, Thailand and the UK, are wisely only in the fray for one of the two big elections to international legal bodies scheduled for 2017.

Since we have not heard back, I raise the issue with anyone and everyone during my visit to India in September 2016. 'Of course, we are not planning to contest the ICJ,' is the reassuring response from External Affairs Minister Sushma Swaraj. 'You focus on the outcomes of the two important elections on your plate. They are enough for now,' she says. Armed with such assurances, we plunge into the efforts being made to ensure victories for Dr Rajput and Dr Chadha.

Soon after, I encounter Judge Bhandari for the first time when he requests to meet me in New York in October 2016.

Having grown up with an enormous regard for the higher Indian judiciary, I am pleasantly surprised that the judge wants to come over and meet me while on a visit to New York.

Judge Bhandari has impressive credentials. Born soon after Independence, on 1 October 1947, he is from a family of lawyers in Rajasthan. Following his early practice there, he was a judge of the Delhi High Court from March 1991 to July 2004 and Chief Justice of the Bombay High Court from July 2004 to October 2005 before being elevated to the Supreme Court of India in October 2005. During his tenure at the highest Indian court, Judge Bhandari's judgements brought about several welfare measures, including night shelters for homeless persons, providing food grain to those living below the poverty line, and improving infrastructure in primary and secondary schools. He was serving there until his election to the ICJ in April 2012.

At my first meeting, the extraordinary graciousness and humility with which Judge Bhandari carries himself is what strikes me most. More than scholarly or erudite, he comes across as grounded and understanding of the harsh realities of everyday life. Extremely soft-spoken and polite to a fault, he is nevertheless sharply focused on seeking re-election. Speaking in chaste Hindi, in an understated manner, he enquires: 'What is my fate?'

Rather than being drawn into matters which are well beyond my pay grade, I assume a deadpan demeanour and respond, 'Please seek the answers in New Delhi. That is where such decisions are made, and that is where these matters are decided. We only implement what is decided there.' Not one to give up easily, he persists in his low-key manner.

'Answers are not forthcoming,' he acknowledges as I accompany him to the mission's huge brass doorway at the end of the meeting. Peering through his horn-rimmed spectacles, he is hoping for some clues from me. I evade his query and instead draw his attention to the craftsmanship and distinctive style of the doors made in his home state of Rajasthan which have become quite an attraction for visitors, many of whom are usually found posing for photographs in front of them. Some even term the location 'Indiana Jones and the Temple of Doom'. Judge Bhandari recognizes my response for what it is—a diversionary tactic—and probes no further.

The incumbent clearly has re-election on his mind. However, as his potential campaign team, we have been directed to focus on other issues. Meanwhile, the other protagonists and teams from five countries have the field to themselves and are busy canvassing for votes amongst UN members. That sums up the situation of our candidacy to the ICJ in 2016.

In November 2016, Dr Rajput polls more votes than any other Indian candidate in the seventy-year history of the ILC (established in 1947).[15] He tops the score sheet amongst all ten candidates elected from Asia, garnering 160 of the 191 valid votes, ahead of many other distinguished jurists who have usually polled much higher than Indian candidates in the past.[16] It is simple; it shows that what is of consequence is how much India matters to the UN membership, not the internal bickering amongst ourselves about who India's candidate is.

Sunday, 1 January – Sunday, 30 April 2017
New York and New Delhi

On 22 and 23 January 2017, we have our annual meeting for UN matters in New York with all the senior officials dealing with the UN in New Delhi. We deliberate on goals for the year and work out plans for our activities during the year, including all elections. The ICJ election is not one of the dozen priorities we agree upon as our objectives at the UN for the year; the election to the ITLOS is, and we were keen to ensure that Dr Chadha does well.

Come February 2017, there are stirrings; we are asked to send an updated analysis of the ICJ situation. This comes as a surprise. It is almost a year since we sent our first detailed assessment on the ICJ and have followed it up with several further updates and in-person discussions. Some key personnel have changed both in New Delhi and New York. Noor Rahman has left for Jeddah, where he is now India's Consul General. Nevertheless, Tanmaya, who is a repository of information on the subject, marshals all facts at our disposal to argue that it is too late for us to enter the fray. If facts can win an argument, then there is no case for launching a campaign almost a year after the others have.

On my visit to India in March 2017, the matter is raised repeatedly at several meetings. External Affairs Minister Sushma Swaraj, India's first woman in the position, is a leading Bharatiya Janata Party (BJP) figure in the political firmament, having served as the Leader of the Opposition in the lower house of Parliament, the Lok Sabha. In that capacity, she has met all visiting heads of state and government during official tours as it is customary to have such courtesy meetings. Not only is she knowledgeable about global issues but is also familiar with many global leaders. She is a diligent minister who is very hands-on in assessing the viability of any option. I recollect that soon after she became its minister, the Ministry of External Affairs set up a twenty-four-hour control room to respond to queries about Indians being evacuated from Iraq in 2014. She personally phoned all the helplines listed at different times, without disclosing her identity, and found that the listed phone line wasn't functional and some staff were not briefed well enough to respond to even common queries. Being a lawyer, she always probes deeply and examines matters threadbare. She usually consults many diplomats who have previously handled similar issues and gauges the political temperature of colleagues from across the spectrum before finally making up her mind about issues.

The internal dynamics beyond diplomatic considerations involved in decision-making are brought home to me during one of the conversations that I am asked to join. A functionary from the ruling dispensation argues, 'Why is there reticence when at the last election the former government was able to place its candidate in the ICJ?' Another adds sharply, 'What use is the Ministry of External Affairs if it cannot convert the huge domestic goodwill into international dividends?'

At the minister's behest, I explain our historical record in ICJ elections at some length, drawing extensively upon the information gleaned by our officials who have dug deep to compile a treasure trove of details about Indian candidates contesting the ICJ. We have won three elections to a full term at the ICJ in five attempts. These were by Dr B.N. Rau (1951)[17] and Dr Nagendra Singh (1972 and 1981).[18] On the other hand, we have lost two elections to a full term of the ICJ contested by Dr B.N. Rau (1948)[19] and Dr Nagendra Singh (1969).[20] The persistence of Dr Rau and Dr Singh three years after their initial losses was a factor in their later successes.

In addition, we have also contested three times in what can be termed as a 'bye-election', when a judge had either died or resigned. In two cases, it was when Indian incumbents had died. In one case, Judge Radhabinod Pal (1954) lost to Pakistan's Sir Muhammad Zafrullah Khan to fill the vacancy arising from Dr B.N. Rau's death.[21] In another case, Judge R.S. Pathak won the 1989 election to complete the less than two years left over from Judge Nagendra Singh's incomplete term.[22]

In fact, following the only case of victory in a bye-election due to the death of an Indian incumbent judge on the ICJ in 1989, we did not support Judge Pathak. He had served as the Chief Justice of the Supreme Court and was keen to re-contest when the subsequent election to a full term was held in 1990. Instead, India supported Sri Lanka's Judge Christopher Gregory Weeramantry, who won.[23] Judge Bhandari (2012) had won the seat[24] for the remainder of the term, replacing Judge Awn Shawkat Al-Khasawneh[25] of Jordan, who had resigned. Hence, I explain, 'the current situation we are confronted with is not comparable with the earlier experience of 2012'. It is unparalleled. Never before has an Indian judge who had contested a bye election then contested for a full term upon completion of the initial limited term. This time, if we contest, we will not only go against all past precedents but will face a very difficult situation, as we are at least a year behind the others in even declaring our interest in fielding a candidate, let alone announcing one.

I remind them that the four other sitting judges who are due to complete their term are actively canvassing for support. The fifth candidate, Ambassador Nawaf Salam from the Asia-Pacific, has, over the course of his long campaign, already garnered public support from the Arab group, the OIC Group (Organization of Islamic Cooperation) and the Francophonie (French-speaking states), which added up to almost ninety of the 193 members of the UN. Nawaf has been making the argument to the fifty-four states of the OIC that proportional representation requires three judges from OIC states, as against merely two (from Morocco and Somalia) who are currently on the ICJ. To other small states, he projects the need for periodic rotation as the only way small states could get a chance. To the Arab and the Francophonie groups, the need for one of their own is compelling. These have ensured considerable support for him well before we have even contemplated our candidature.

'Given an even playing field, we can easily win. However, not deciding on our candidature for a year has left us at a major disadvantage as others have been playing the field for long,' I plead. UN elections are also transactional in nature and we have exhausted opportunities for tie-ups with others as we have used them in two elections to other legal bodies, while the others have planned better and remained focused on their objective of a seat on the ICJ.

I hope the rationale offered is adequate to explain the nuances of our present situation. While there is understanding of the views expressed, I realize that the political equations at play are well beyond my ken. Political queries require political answers—not long, reasoned responses.

I am grateful to the redoubtable Sushma Swaraj's political skills in navigating such matters. She does so with remarkable dexterity. 'If, as some of you say, the judge is a nominee of the earlier dispensation, why are we arguing amongst ourselves to favour him now with another term? Let us end this needless discussion,' she asserts firmly, concluding the conversation.

Armed with the certainty that the reiteration of a 'no' from the external affairs minister has ended the debate, I return to New York. Our goal is still to ensure a huge victory for Dr Chadha at the ITLOS election on the lines of Dr Rajput's success at the ILC. Judge Bhandari's candidacy is no longer on the anvil. When queried if we are not being overly ambitious by contesting all three elections to legal fora, we repeatedly assure interlocutors that we have not announced re-election to the ICJ, and it is not on the horizon.

Monday, 8 May 2017
New York

Throwing away years of unwillingness to engage the ICJ, India approaches it against the decision of a Pakistani military court to execute Indian national Kulbhushan Sudhir Jadhav.[26]

India claims that Pakistan had failed to inform it, without delay, of the arrest and detention of Jadhav. It further contends that Jadhav had not been informed of his rights under the Vienna Convention on Consular Relations.[27] Indian consular officers had been denied access to Jadhav while he was in custody, detention and prison, and had been unable to converse and correspond with him or arrange for his legal representation. India, therefore, accuses Pakistan of actions in violation of its multilateral commitments under the Vienna Convention of Consular Relations and invokes the Statute of the ICJ and the Optional Protocol of the Vienna Convention for seeking compulsory settlement of the dispute at the ICJ.

The carefully crafted plea has cloaked the Indian request squarely in terms of a multilateral agreement rather than any bilateral treaty. It argues that Pakistan was violating its multilateral commitments and seeks the intervention of the multilateral judicial institution to remedy this. This is new. Usually, India has been reticent in approaching international institutions, preferring to address issues bilaterally. On this occasion, India does not follow conventional wisdom. While not eschewing bilateralism in ties with Pakistan, India finds a way to pursue its interest differently. It displays a willingness to proactively engage multilateral institutions in pursuit of national benefit. It also signals a willingness to tread unconventional paths and take risks.

Monday, 15 May–Monday, 22 May 2017
New York

Responding to India's request, the ICJ convenes swiftly, holds public hearings on 15 May and orders 'provisional measures' on 18 May.[28] Pakistan is directed to take all measures at its disposal to ensure that Kulbhushan Jadhav is not executed pending a final decision in the case, and to inform the court of all the measures taken in implementation.

The swift judicial intervention enables decision-makers in India to see the ICJ in a different light. It is no longer an institution in a faraway land with little direct relevance to key Indian interests. It is now a crucial battleground in an important diplomatic tussle. It is no longer of little interest to India's vital national interests.

Having a judge on the ICJ is not a matter any longer of weighing the validity of various arguments. India's interests require a judge on the court. Every state which has a case before the court is eligible to have an ad hoc judge. However, our stakes are such that vacating a full-time seat of an elected judge and instead settling for an ad hoc one for the case will be a comedown hard to justify. To me, it seems that the requirements of realpolitik will tilt the argument towards the need for India to contest the election.

As diplomats at the UN, we are well aware that while the ICJ Statute, on paper, goes to considerable lengths to reduce the influence of politics on the ICJ, in practice this is not always the case. For example, Article 2 of the ICJ Statute calls for 'a body of independent judges, elected irrespective of their nationality from among persons of high moral character, who possess the qualifications required in their respective countries for appointment to the highest judicial offices, or are jurisconsults of recognized competence in international law'.[29]

However, the 'regardless of their nationality' test was never applied whenever nominees of the permanent members of the Security Council were in the fray during the seventy-year history of the United Nations. Their permanent presence in the ICJ, though not specified in the Statute of the court, is the norm. The rest of the current 188 members have to make do and contest for the remaining ten seats in accordance with a primitive unwritten scheme that recognized geopolitical status and nothing else. Since this is so, the new orientation towards the ICJ that we are pursuing, as reflected in the Jadhav case, will inexorably lead to the idea that if the interests of the permanent members demanded they had a permanent presence, so did our growing interests and changing orientation and engagement towards the ICJ.

To me, it is apparent that it is only a matter of time before the rationality of the reasoning for a 'no, not now' yields to the reality of veering towards a 'yes, we need an Indian judge on the ICJ'. The long journey from 'no' to 'yes' is reaching its final denouement.

2

Come with a Plan, Not as a Plaintiff

Tuesday, 23 May 2017
New York

FOREIGN POLICY DECISIONS don't always come wrapped as neat options prepared on the basis of projections made after substantial research and careful consideration. Many times, they entail choices between sub-optimal options that make decision-making difficult. As decisions on inter-state matters relate primarily to an external environment, even the most decisive of decision-makers tend to be cautious. With authority and influence beyond national borders being diffused, the limits of power, when combined with the complexity of domestic inputs and dynamics, can often make for a tortuous decision-making process.

With national prestige being involved, risk aversion is the default option. However, a swift 'no' in a well-oiled decision-making process can often be incorrectly characterized, especially in hindsight, as lacking adequate application of mind. Hence, 'careful consideration', bureaucratese for putting the matter on the back burner, is not an uncommon recourse. If it reinforces the initial 'nay', then all ends well. However, if the process meanders and then, for any reason, results in a reversal of the conventional wisdom of a 'no' with a 'risk worth taking yes', then the real challenge begins.

For me, this challenge begins today. Like Indian diplomats globally, we, in New York, too are following the developments in the Jadhav case closely. The extensive coverage of the case in the media means a wider swathe of Indians are gaining a better understanding of the role and importance of the ICJ. To us, it appears inevitable that the changed circumstances will mean a review of the decision to give up our seat on the ICJ when Judge Bhandari's term ends in November 2017. For a few days now, some of us have been thinking that another election is looming large in the near future. Yet, all of us at the mission in New York are going about the goal of garnering votes for Dr Chadha's candidature to the ITLOS with gusto. It isn't a case of living in denial. It reflects the discipline of a determined group pursuing an agreed goal, to the exclusion of all else.

May is a busy month. Activities at the UN are in full swing. Our campaign for Dr Chadha's election is proceeding smoothly. She has visited New York twice. In the company of our ebullient election officer Anjani Kumar and newly arrived legal adviser Umasankar, she has met most delegations to pursue her candidature. The rest of us are all lobbying for her case individually with other diplomats at various levels.

As I end a meeting at the UN headquarters and saunter back to the mission, enjoying the pleasant mid-morning New York weather, my phone buzzes. It is Foreign Secretary Dr S. Jaishankar from Delhi. As always, he comes to the point immediately. 'I am giving you a telephonic heads-up. A formal message will follow. You are required in Delhi for urgent consultations on the ICJ elections.' Aware of my oft-repeated view that the ICJ race is now a no-win situation for us, he tactfully conveys the message that things have changed.

'Come with a plan and not as a plaintiff,' he advises. 'Other options are no longer on the table. By the time you come to Delhi, you should have a battle plan ready as we will be required to announce a candidate soon,' he concludes and signs off without providing scope for any further discussion.

Thursday, 25 May 2017
Mid-air, en route to New Delhi from New York

On the long-haul New York–New Delhi Air India flight, rummaging through the material prepared for my visit by all the officers, I come across Robert Kolb's monograph on the ICJ. My long-time personal assistant, Vaidyanathan, seems to have sensed the primary purpose of the visit and has helpfully added it to the reading material. The book is a useful refresher course in understanding the ICJ.

The ICJ is the principal judicial organ of the UN. It is organically linked to the UN through references in Articles 7(1) and 92 of the UN Charter. The Statute of the ICJ, based on the statute of its predecessor, the Permanent Court of International Justice (PCIJ), which was part of the League of Nations system, is annexed to the UN's Charter.

Located in The Hague, the ICJ is situated far away from the political nerve centre of New York. Yet, elections to the fifteen-member court, usually held once every three years to fill five vacancies, ensure that the political flavour of New York is never entirely lost in its composition. Also, it used to be the only principal organ that did not present a report to the General Assembly, ostensibly to keep it away from the political issues. Since 1968, though, the ICJ president presents an annual report to apprise the broader UN membership of developments in the field of international law. The practice of the ICJ president briefing the Security Council and interacting with its members in a private meeting during visits to New York has also evolved. To sum up: while judicially independent, the ICJ is an integral part of the UN system.

Elections to the ICJ are complex. They follow a devilishly arcane system adopted from the practice of elections to the PCIJ. They are conducted by secret ballot, simultaneously but separately in two bodies of the UN—the General Assembly (193 members) and the Security Council (fifteen members). Candidates have to be elected by both bodies.

There is no formal distribution of seats. Article 9 of the ICJ Statute requires representation of the 'main forms of civilization and of the principal legal systems of the world'. In practice, the court's composition reflects that of the Security Council. Each of the five permanent members have always had a judge on the bench. The remaining ten judges follow geographical distribution as in the Security Council. That is: African states have three, Latin American and the Caribbean states two, Asian states two, Western European and other states two, and Eastern European states one.

Winners are not declared based only on the highest number of votes polled (as is the case in the 'first past the post' system followed in elections to the US Congress or the Indian Lok Sabha). Reaching above a threshold (say a two-thirds majority of votes cast, as in the election to the UN Security Council's non-permanent membership) also does not ensure success. In the contest for five seats, only when five candidates achieve the requisite threshold of 'absolute majority' of ninety-seven votes in the General Assembly are their names compared with the five candidates who have obtained the 'absolute majority' of eight votes in the Security Council. Those who figure in both lists are then declared winners.

In other words, the election cannot be won only by crossing thresholds. For example, when five seats are contested, if six candidates obtain the absolute majority, then the five with the highest votes are not considered to have won. Instead, balloting will continue for all the candidates until just five candidates get the absolute majority. When this happens, those who have obtained the absolute majority in both bodies are declared elected. Another ballot will take place for the remaining seat/s if less than five names are common in the lists of the outcomes in both bodies. This ensuing ballot will be restricted to the remaining candidates. If necessary, repeated ballots will be held, until the requisite number of candidates obtain the absolute majority in both bodies.

The more I wrestle with the task of understanding the nuances of the ICJ's electoral process on this thirteen-hour flight from New York to New Delhi, the greater is my self-flagellation for the enormous efforts we put in elections to other legal bodies over the last twelve months and not this one. In retrospect, I feel that it may not have been in our long-term interests. Other states have adopted a calibrated strategy to keep their resources ready for major battles rather than involving themselves in multiple electoral skirmishes. For example, France grasped the increasingly transactional nature of elections at the UN following the failure of its candidate, Mathias Forteau, to get elected to the ILC in 2016.[1] After that, it offered reciprocal support to us, tying up its ICJ with our ITLOS candidature and we gladly accepted it as, at that stage, we did not have the ICJ election as an objective. Subsequently, it even withdrew from the race for the Human Rights Council[2] to be held ahead of the ICJ election in 2017 to focus primarily on its ICJ candidature. On the other hand, we are planning an effort to win the most difficult election known to multilateral diplomacy after having used up our resources in two other elections to legal bodies. No one else has ventured on the path that we are now set to pursue.

There is no point in agitating about bygone matters. You go to battle with what you have, not with what you want. We now need a game plan for the future which steers clear of any resemblance to a plaintiff pleading for a lost cause.

⚬⚬⚬

Friday, 26 May 2017
New Delhi

As I land in Delhi around 4 p.m. and switch on my smartphone, I notice a message from Apoorva Srivastava, the foreign service officer and point person in the external affairs minister's office. I am informed that the minister wants to meet me at 8 p.m. at her residence along with Foreign Secretary Dr Jaishankar. It is a Friday evening but Sushma Swaraj is never one to delay matters or stand on protocol. Once she decides, she prefers moving swiftly on official business.

When I get to the minister's residence at 8 Safdarjung Lane, in the heart of Lutyens' Delhi, her staff tells me that the foreign secretary is delayed a bit and will join soon but the minister is ready to meet me. The frugally furnished meeting room at the minister's residence holds memories of many meetings and decisions that I was part of as the Official

Spokesperson of the Ministry of External Affairs. As usual, Swaraj is well prepared. She informs me about the background to the decision. 'Everyone is aware of your view that given an even playing field, we can win; but now the dice is loaded against us,' she acknowledges. 'However, circumstances have changed. Consequently, plans have to change too,' she adds disarmingly. 'I was with you when we discussed the ICJ in the past. Now you need to be with me,' she frames her response with remarkable candour and goes on to explain the changed situation resulting in the change of plans, the importance of the ICJ to our current way of thinking and the necessity of contesting the election in November.

Of her own accord, she mentions, 'Serious consideration was given to the choice of the candidate. There were other names in the mix, including some who are still serving on the Supreme Court. On balance, it was felt that the situation is too fragile to rock the boat now. Therefore, Judge Bhandari will be our nominee.'

Since the ICJ nominee is formally to be put forth by the National Group of India, they have had informal consultations and are scheduled to meet in early June to confirm the understanding that they evolved during consultations. The circuitous nomination process through the National Group— which, in India, now consists of Justice H.L. Dattu (former Chief Justice of India and Chairperson of the National Human Rights Commission), Justice G.T. Nanavati (former judge of the Supreme Court of India), Attorney General Mukul Rohatgi and senior advocate Harish Salve—is a mechanism that was adopted by the ICJ from its predecessor, the PCIJ. It provides for a broader basis than only the executive in the selection of the nominee. So, technically, the candidate is a nominee of the National Group, rather than of the government.

Whatever may be the rationale for our decision, the ICJ is an independent judicial body; hence we agree to keep our case limited to the judicial issues: the abiding faith that we have in international law, the strong common law tradition in India, the merits of the Indian candidate and his contributions during his current tenure on the court, which is less than a normal nine-year term.

During the course of the conversation, Foreign Secretary Dr Jaishankar joins in and adroitly steers the discussion to focus on the specific needs that require addressing and concrete plans that have to be implemented over the next few months.

Given the large number of countries and our diplomatic outreach, we will be fully stretched over the next few months trying to catch up. We have a diplomatic presence in 117 countries. This leaves seventy-five where we have no resident missions. As every vote counts, apart from New York, we will need to reach out in the capitals of every country. This is a task which requires coordination from our headquarters. Despite the difficulties, we feel that it is feasible to get an absolute majority in the General Assembly.

To strengthen coordination at the headquarters, an officer is deputed with the responsibility of working full-time on the election in addition to the UN divisions, which usually handle such matters. Vinod Jacob, the director handling Pakistan, is chosen as the point person. He has previously served in New York and understands the situation at both the New York and Delhi ends. The mission in New York is being strengthened with the temporary deployment of Paulomi Tripathi, who will be leaving behind her key personnel responsibilities in the ministry and two young children in Delhi to rush to New York.

We have a good track record of winning elections. This is primarily on account of our choosing carefully, planning well and campaigning long and hard. On this occasion, our conventional approach cannot be followed in full measure. We need to, therefore, pull out all the stops to gain support—not only in New York but in all key capitals, especially those of Security Council members. Dr Jaishankar agrees that every one of the Council members will be approached individually at the highest possible level, including during summits such as the forthcoming Shanghai Cooperation Organization (SCO) Summit in Astana, where India is due to join as a full member in June 2017.[3] Additionally, designated special envoys will visit all members of the Council to pursue their support.

Our weakness in starting late will make it difficult to woo the members of the Security Council adequately. With just fifteen members, our prospect of gathering an absolute majority of eight is daunting. Adding to this is the fact that two of the permanent members have candidates who will benefit from the unwritten understanding that all of the so-called P-5 will vote for each other in any ICJ election, thereby starting with the assurance that they already have five of the eight votes needed for an absolute majority. This has ensured that the P-5 nominees are always elected to the ICJ. Also, although the rules do not provide for a regional distribution of seats, given the distribution of seats on the Council, it is assumed that Council members elected from a region will normally vote for candidates from that region. Asia alone has two candidates, and the Indian candidate begins with the disadvantage of starting more than a year after the other. All this requires high-level attention, since the stakes are very high. Even with all these plans, our collective conclusion is that 'the Council may be our Achilles heel'.

Tuesday, 30 May 2017
Mid-air, en route to New York from New Delhi

Dr Jaishankar summoned all the key personnel of the ministry handling multilateral issues—including Ruchi Ghanashyam, who has been our High Commissioner in South Africa in the past and has recently taken over as Secretary (West) with responsibility for the UN—to his residence on the morning of Sunday, 28 May. He briefed us about the decision to contest the ICJ election and the importance of starting our campaign as soon as the National Group decides upon the nomination. Upon my request, he agreed that we will formally file the nomination in New York only after the election to the ITLOS, which is scheduled for mid-June. This will ensure that our campaign for the ITLOS in New York is not adversely affected. However, it was agreed that we can begin to discretely campaign in various capitals, across the globe, a week before we file our formal nomination.

The next day, I made the usual rounds to meet ministers and other senior officials in Delhi on various issues. The ICJ election came up in some discussions. A senior official mischievously questioned me, 'What is your exit strategy from this disaster?' 'None,' was my candid confession. It is a fight that I would not have picked. However, now that we are in it, there is only one way out for me—a successful outcome.

A little later, a minister holding an important portfolio, whom I met on another matter, reprimanded me for putting the 'nation's prestige at stake in such a risky venture for the sake of the glory of the Ministry of External Affairs'. It is a no-win situation. Damned if you don't, damned if you do.

Such exchanges are par for the course when difficult situations are to be faced. There are those who put their heart and soul into a fight. And then there are those who try to pin the blame on others or make a safe exit even before the fight has begun. As a foot soldier used to fighting in the trenches, it is important for me to shut these thoughts out and get ready for the forthcoming fight.

3

Big and Small—All Are in the Fray

———⚬⚬⚬———

Wednesday, 14 June 2017
New York

B EFORE WE LAUNCH the ICJ campaign in New York, there
is still a matter that needs to be settled. We are in the final
phases of the ITLOS campaign for Dr Neeru Chadha. ITLOS is
an independent judicial body established by the United Nations
Convention on the Law of the Sea (UNCLOS) to adjudicate
disputes arising out of the interpretation and application of the
Convention.

Since the inception of the twenty-one-member Tribunal in
1996, India has always been represented on it. Dr Chadha is
contesting to fill the vacancy on account of former Law Secretary
Dr P. Chandrasekhara Rao completing his term. There are two
seats allocated for the Asia-Pacific region and four candidates
are in the fray. Ambassador Joseph Akl (Lebanon) has been a
member since 1996 and is seeking re-election. Ambassadors
Kriangsak Kittichaisaree (Thailand) and Arif Havas Oegroseno
(Indonesia) are the other candidates.

Like at the ICJ, members of the ITLOS serve for nine years
and one-third of the members are elected every three years.
To be elected, a candidate needs to get the largest number of
votes, including a two-thirds majority of the states present

and voting. Multi-cornered contests for multiple seats are unpredictable if they go into multiple rounds. Our objective is to win in the first round. It means that we need to get about a third of all the votes cast in a strong field of four candidates, each with excellent legal credentials. It is a tough ask. However, we have started early, planned well, worked hard and are hoping for success.

Early in the morning, all of us swarm into the overflowing Conference Room One. It is lodged deep in the underbelly of the General Assembly building and is one of the favoured locations for conducting meetings that require balloting. The tables are covered with portfolios of candidates along with gift pens, keychains, chocolate boxes and other goodies. It is a practice that we have objected to, and the General Assembly has agreed to put a stop to from the next session, which will start in September 2017.

Our early scouts note that one African state does not have its representative present even though they sent in their credentials a day earlier. For us, this means that a committed voter is not in the room. My younger colleagues make some frantic calls, but to no avail. The diplomat who is to vote is being held up on account of a delay on the Long Island Rail Road service. The assessment is that he will not make it in time. An enthusiastic new colleague rushes in with a suggestion: send a car to pick the diplomat up. Another, who has been in New York for a longer duration, takes a quick look at Google Maps and exclaims, 'We can't pick anyone up from Far Rockaway and bring them to Turtle Bay in less than half an hour.' The idea is nipped in the bud.

The voting starts on time. It is conducted smoothly and completed early in the morning session. The results exceed our hopes. Of the 166 votes cast, one is invalid. The threshold of two-thirds for winning in the first round is 110. Dr Chadha gets 120 votes. This is thirty-four votes more than her nearest opponent, Thailand's Ambassador Kriangsak Kittichaisaree, who garners 86. Lebanon's serving member, Ambassador Joseph Akl, polls only 60 votes, with Indonesia's Ambassador Arif Oegroseno coming in last with 58. Dr Chadha's tally is the highest for an Indian in an election at the ITLOS. She is the first Indian woman to be elected to an international judicial body, and only the second woman member in the history of the ITLOS.[1] Later in the afternoon, Ambassador Kittichaisaree wins the other seat from the Asia-Pacific region. Our job is done, but there is no time to savour the victory.

The need to shift focus to the ICJ rapidly is driven home to me soon after. The reminder comes from an unexpected quarter. The Permanent Representative of Uzbekistan, who recently joined in New York, Ambassador Bakhtiyor Ibragimov, wants to meet at short notice. As our missions are located just across the street from each other, he comes over in a jiffy. After a brief introduction, he explains the catalyst for the meeting. 'Prime Minister Modi met our President Shavkat Mirziyoyev on the fringes of the SCO Summit in Astana. Following their conversation and the understanding reached between them, I have instructions from the President's office to immediately confirm support for the Indian candidate for the ICJ,' he confides in hushed tones. While gratefully accepting the first written confirmation of support, I sheepishly respond, 'We are yet to formally submit Judge Bhandari's nomination.' These short interactions of leaders, on the fringes of summits, tend to yield more than what meets the eye.

The diplomatic note that Ambassador Ibragimov handed over to me makes for interesting reading. It contains an affirmation of support by Uzbekistan for India's candidate to the ICJ. No name is provided, as none has been formally announced. It drives home to me the importance being placed by leaders on the Indian candidature to the ICJ. Following suit with the same alacrity and gusto is what is expected of us.

In the evening, after reviewing the ITLOS results, I share the news with my colleagues. 'We already have a confirmation even before we, in New York, have begun to seek votes for the ICJ.' Judging from their startled reactions, I understand that the efforts being put in pursuit of Judge Bhandari's candidature are having an impact on them too. In the past, elections were primarily driven by our mission in New York. The efforts were merely supplemented by the headquarters and our missions abroad. However, this time it is an all-out effort from the word go. Big and small—indeed all in the Indian foreign policy firmament are engaged in this campaign from the outset. Our spirits are boosted. We are all geared up for the long and tough path ahead.

Monday, 19 June 2017
New York

Following the formal decision of the Indian National Group to nominate Judge Bhandari, we submitted his candidature papers to the UN Secretariat earlier today. At the UN, news travels fast. Since we are all set to move ahead, I phone the ambassadors of the six other countries already in the fray to inform them of our decision as a courtesy. Yes, five has become six. Zambia has decided that Judge Chaloka Beyani[2] of their Constitutional Court will be a candidate even before we announced that Judge Bhandari is in the fray.

Over the course of the last two elections, we have put in place a good mechanism to reach out to all missions in New York. It is multi-layered. All UN members are distributed amongst the diplomatic officers of the mission. Usually, it means that each diplomat reaches out to twelve or fifteen members. Each diplomat engages with these interlocutors regularly over a period of time and provides an update every week. Tanmaya and I distribute the senior ambassadors amongst ourselves. Each of us is responsible for reaching out to about 100 Permanent Representatives or Deputy Permanent Representatives. This way, we have at least a two-tiered view of what each delegation is thinking in New York. This is supplemented by information from Delhi and from various capitals.

The election officer, Counsellor Anjani Kumar—Anjani to all of us—is the anchor person. His ebullient personality and camera skills have made him a popular figure in the election officers' community. This close-knit group is an interesting one. Each election officer is pursuing very specific national interests, pushing unique requirements, exchanging information, cutting quiet deals and looking to maximize support for national candidatures. Collectively they are a visible presence at most UN events. Group dynamics ensure that they are in constant touch and temper sharp divergences, even in circumstances of acute competition and fierce national rivalry. Popularly known as the 'selfie man', on account of his ability to take selfies of large groups of forty to fifty people, Anjani is a ubiquitous figure at the election events of every mission. Notwithstanding that we have a very accomplished election officer at the Indian mission, every diplomatic officer also shoulders limited election-related responsibilities pertaining to the countries they are to engage with, in addition to their other work. It is possible that some may not be happy with this arrangement as they are repeatedly asked to reach out to reluctant interlocutors to get clarity. But in due course, as disciplined officials, they invariably recognize these responsibilities as intrinsic to their normal work. This system helps all of us to understand the situation better, taking into account diverse perspectives and interesting aspects that are placed on the table from different sources. It also helps each of our diplomats to move out of the comfort zones of the silos they are otherwise required to burrow themselves in, so as to understand the complexity of the issues they are handling individually. Finally, it enables all of us to work together on a common goal with a defined outcome.

This 'All of Mission' approach towards elections and other issues at the UN stems from my own difficult experience as a younger officer at the UN in the 1990s. Those were times when it was generally believed that senior officials were the ones who decided regarding voting; we younger officers were peripheral to the election effort. Neither were we called upon to intensely engage with others nor was the information we gleaned considered entirely reliable. Thus, as far as elections were concerned, we were on the fringes; our seniors held fort and worked with our missions globally. Our loss in 1996, by a huge margin, to Japan in the Security Council election left a searing impact on me. Given my chance to lead now, I make it a point to repeatedly emphasize that elections are too serious a business to be left to senior officers only. They impact everyone and so should involve everyone. Everyone needs to fulfil election responsibilities, even if some find it onerous. This includes our

Military Adviser, Colonel Sandeep Kapoor, who was deputed from the Special Forces. To the credit of each of my colleagues, they never shirk their responsibilities or display any resentment towards my persistent hectoring, whatever they may have felt in their hearts. Their work ethic is absolutely professional.

The plan, this time, is to engage with every one of the 192 delegations twice before the summer break in August. It is normal for most interlocutors to merely listen the first time a matter is raised with them. The second meeting within a month or so is designed to convey keenness beyond the usual and get feedback. Schedules are to be worked out by Counsellor Anjani Kumar to ensure there is no overlap and timelines are met. Tanmaya, in consultation with the two joint secretaries at the Ministry of External Affairs handling UN matters—Rudrendra Tandon and Manish Chauhan—along with Director Vinod Jacob, who is the designated point person, will work on the 'talking points' or 'sales pitch' to be used globally. The wheels of Indian diplomacy are moving all over the world—bar Pakistan, from whom we do not intend seeking support.

Tuesday, 20 June – Monday, 31 July 2017
New York

After the buoyant start with a written confirmation of support, the news trickling in during our first forays is grim. Most delegations we approach are polite. They listen carefully and usually respond that they will report to their capitals. Several, who are more candid, mention that those canvassing for the others have been engaging with them at least since mid-2016, a year ahead of us. Some ask: 'Why have you left it till so late to decide on the candidature?' A few acknowledge that they are already committed to some or several candidates. Tanmaya and Anjani, who collate responses and send daily updates, are visibly disconcerted with the responses. As individuals, they are very different from each other. Tanmaya is calm and inscrutable. Anjani, on the other hand, wears his heart on his sleeve. Both seem to agree that we are in a difficult situation.

The replies we receive from our headquarters are more positive than the feedback we are discerning in New York. The replies are largely based on inputs from our missions in other countries and from diplomats of other countries based in Delhi (the latter in case of countries that have resident missions in India although we do not have diplomatic outposts in their capitals). Many acknowledge the need for continuity of the judge, who has not even completed a full term. Some are forthright in expressing support. Others point to the strength of ties to suggest that the candidature will receive 'positive consideration'.

All this is in addition to Prime Minister Narendra Modi raising the issue during bilateral interactions on the sidelines of the G20 Summit in July in Hamburg. Supplementing these interactions are telephonic conversations by External Affairs Minister Sushma Swaraj and the two ministers of state, General (retd.) V.K. Singh and M.J. Akbar. Foreign Secretary Jaishankar and the other secretaries in the Ministry of External Affairs are also pursuing the candidature in regular interactions with their counterparts, whenever and wherever they meet. It is a 'full court press'.

Since, in effect, we are essentially contesting two elections—in the General Assembly and the Security Council—different officials are designated to focus on the responses from the

Security Council as the fifteen of them have two votes each (in the Assembly and the Council).[3]

Joint Secretary Rudrendra Tandon—Rudru to all of us—who is piloting the Council-related activities at the headquarters is sceptical about our chances there. He has studied Judge Bhandari's judgements and found that some members of the Council may be less than satisfied with them. Previously, we had not paid attention to this aspect.

Once Judge Bhandari had joined the ICJ, in the tradition of an independent judge, he had taken stances and written individual judgements. None of us had followed this track. However, those affected seem not to forget. Our initial concerns about gaining an absolute majority in the Security Council are now being given concrete substance by Rudru's and Vinod Jacob's analyses in Delhi.

At the end of a month of intense lobbying, we have reached out to as many as 160 delegations. The initial responses are below par. Estimates, independently compiled by us and our colleagues in Delhi, indicate that we have affirmative responses from about thirty-five countries to show for this hectic effort. Our assessment in New York is a little lower, and that from Delhi a bit higher. The differences are minor. Both assessments indicate that most states are repeatedly mentioning that we were 'late' in approaching them. They are reluctant to go beyond saying that the candidature is receiving 'due consideration'. We have about three months still available.

Judge Bhandari enters the electoral frame, in New York and New Delhi, in July. Receptions and lunches at which the judge can meet and greet diplomats, and then speak from prepared notes, are the usual mechanisms available to candidates desiring to engage diplomats in large gatherings. The last time he was in the fray, Judge Bhandari was pitched against eighty-four-year-old Justice Florentino Feliciano of the Philippines in a direct contest. It was a bye-election. This time it is different. It is a multi-cornered contest with many candidates, all of whom are ahead in terms of their engagement with other delegations. Many in New York want to also meet the judge in person; they want to seek his views on various issues given the importance they place on the ICJ's decisions.

How does one design a 'sales pitch' for a judge to repeatedly make for his own candidature, when by training and disposition he is used to being above the fray of electoral politics? We decide that it will be best if Tanmaya or I accompany him to each of the individual meetings with the ambassadors or delegations. We will initiate the conversation by recalling our earlier meetings and make the pitch. Then we will leave the judge to respond to any queries that the delegations may have on legal or other matters. It will shield him from the discomfort of making a pitch about his credentials to be re-elected.

Judge Bhandari is in New York at the end of July for about a fortnight. He is understanding of the circumstances. In his usual understated manner, he quickly sizes up the situation and acknowledges, 'This is an entirely different situation from 2012.' At one of our regular meetings, he tells me that last time was 'so much easier'. However, he is eager to be intimately involved and is game for anything we suggest. Over the next two weeks, Judge Bhandari is transformed into 'Candidate Bhandari'. Accompanied by Tanmaya or me, he goes over to numerous missions—many a time trudging from one building to another, depending upon where a delegation has indicated their desire to meet him. From Andorra to the USA, all those who ask for meetings are obliged. Some query him on how

48

he sees the 'ICJ evolving in terms of addressing environmental concerns', others on 'whether the funding for the ICJ is adequate'. He answers these patiently but never beyond the minimum required. I notice that he never lets his guard down or becomes expansive, whatever the occasion. Lunches are arranged for cohesive groups of small states, such as the Pacific islands and the Caribbean states, as are larger receptions for all the Permanent Representatives and election officers.

At every reception, Judge Bhandari is provided a platform to lay out his vision. He uses these opportunities to make 'stump' speeches. He always highlights India's legal tradition and adherence to international law, including its acceptance of the compulsory jurisdiction of the ICJ in conformity with Article 36(2) of the Statute of the court. He invariably recalls examples of his contributions during the more than forty years of association with legal issues and his five-year stint in the ICJ during a time when the court's portfolio of cases had been burgeoning. He explains that on many cases at the ICJ, he has given separate opinions and declarations covering issues such as maritime disputes, whaling in Antarctica, crimes of genocide, delimitation of the continental shelf, nuclear disarmament and financing of terrorism. He always emphasizes the importance of objectivity and impartiality in the ICJ's decision-making process, and usually ends by offering his services 'in case member states find me suitable'. In judicial terms, he comes across as having impeccable credentials.

Alas, there is no mechanism that allows for the collective examination of the merits of individual candidates for the ICJ. Many UN bodies have initiated the mandatory exchange of views of candidates with all members. However, no such set-up is available for the election of judges. Also, there is no scrutiny of whether the candidates measure up to requirements stipulated in the Statute of the court. Given the lack of clear guard rails, elections to the ICJ are never only about the credentials of the candidate. All types of diplomatic factors and forces come into play.

In our case, in addition to the issue of the 'late' entry of Judge Bhandari, there are other complications too. Given the strong ties between India and Israel, the latter confirms support. Ambassador Danny Danon attends a reception for Judge Bhandari and with much fanfare announces, in front of a large number of diplomats, that Israel has nominated Judge Bhandari as its non-national candidate to the ICJ. This immediately sets a whisper campaign in motion. Israel's unprecedented decision to nominate a non-national candidate to the ICJ leads to several of the Arabs, and others with sympathies for the Palestinian cause, being told to be wary of Judge Bhandari's candidature.

All this is happening against the backdrop of the situation in Doklam, at the tri-junction of India, China and Bhutan, where Indian and Chinese troops are involved in a stand-off. Diplomats at the UN tend to link every development with everything else. An ambassador from a small island state asks me, 'What is China's stance on Judge Bhandari's candidature?' The reality is that while usually we had a reasonably good understanding on election matters, this time China is unwilling to consider support for the Indian judge. So all I can do is hedge and say, 'We are in touch and such decisions take time to be decided in their system.' All factually correct and enough to parry such queries.

Also, when judgements of the majority are written as a group, the state which does not gain from the majority decision usually is reconciled as it doesn't identify specificity of views. Judge Bhandari's style of expressing separate opinions and declarations has made his individual opinion on most cases clear. Both he and India abide strictly by the solemn declaration in Article 20 of the ICJ Statute that every member of the court exercise its powers impartially and conscientiously. However, those who feel that Judge Bhandari's rulings are not in their support are finding different ways to express their views. Some allude in general terms that given the ICJ's importance, their legal departments are keeping close track of the judgements and will provide inputs in the final decision-making process. Others are more specific and suggest that we look at the judgements that Judge Bhandari had written before following up with them. When I explain this to Judge Bhandari, he seems worried as well as surprised and queries, 'Doesn't the independence and integrity of judges matter?' As a hard-nosed diplomat, I have no answer except keeping quiet and smiling at such naïveté. What is judicially proper is not always electorally useful. It is left to diplomats to square this circle.

4
Learning from History

Tuesday, 1 August – Saturday, 30 September 2017

AUGUST IS LEAN season at the UN. Judge Bhandari leaves muggy New York in early August after interacting with more than a hundred delegations. He appears to be happy with the large number of ambassadors and delegates who turn up for his reception. For me, attendance at receptions is no barometer of support, so the gnawing doubts remain. Most delegates too have started to leave for their vacations. For us, at the Indian Mission, there is no prospect of holidays in sight. We are so far behind in the race for the ICJ that even thinking of leave is anathema. At the beginning of August, our tally of support is about fifty in the General Assembly and three in the Security Council. We are approximately a third of where we want to be in November. A long period of toil awaits us.

Usually, candidates with impressive judicial credentials seek the support of other countries to get themselves nominated as non-national candidates. Since such support is formally from the National Group of a country and these National Groups inevitably consist of legal luminaries of the country extending support, it enhances the judicial credentials of the candidate—besides adding political weight to the candidature.

All the other sitting judges of the ICJ have burnished their credentials by being able to showcase an impressive list of National Groups willing to support them as non-national candidates. Judge Ronny Abraham, who is serving as the President of the court, has twenty-five National Groups listed in his support. Judge Abdulqawi Ahmed Yusuf of Somalia, who is the Vice President of the court, has twenty-two; Judge Christopher Greenwood of the UK has nineteen; Judge Antônio Augusto Cançado Trindade of Brazil has fifteen. For Judge Bhandari, since the effort took off very late, there are only five (Australia, Bangladesh, Colombia, India and Israel).[1]

Our candidate has the lowest National Groups' support of all the sitting judges. This is unnerving. Before his departure, Judge Bhandari asks, 'What more can I do?' I suggest, 'Reach out to your peers, and get some National Group support.' Despite his efforts, Judge Bhandari's National Group support remains only higher than Nawaf's tally of two (France and Lebanon). However, Nawaf is not a judge. His strategy is not aimed at highlighting his judicial credentials. It is based on a very early start and broad support of various political groups, such as the Arab Group, the OIC and the Francophonie. This political support amounts to nearly ninety states. It is supplemented by individual, reciprocal tie-ups over a long time and extensive personal familiarity with the electoral college, as Nawaf has been one amongst them for more than a decade.

Indian diplomats continue to frequent the regular watering holes at the UN, even though the Vienna Cafe in the UN building and the Delegates Lounge bear a forlorn look, bereft as they are of the usual suspects who frequent these places. Nevertheless, these haunts of UN diplomats, as well as the premises of the numerous permanent missions in mid-town Manhattan, remain regular ports of call for each of us at different times of the day, even in August.

Sometimes, such forays yield dividends. 'There is a propensity to give more importance to the Security Council. You keep your focus on the General Assembly,' is the sage advice of Jamaica's widely respected Ambassador Earle Courtenay Rattray as he recounts his experience of the ICJ elections of 2014. In the course of an expansive conversation, Ambassador Rattray explains with a lot of passion how a Jamaican judge had won a prolonged election then. 'It may be well worth your while to study that outcome in more detail,' he says, concluding the most useful piece of advice I have got so far. I hold on to that nugget for dear life.

Later, during my usual sharing of the day's experiences with Tanmaya, as a precursor to his daily dispatch, he too feels this needs to be explored further. We task Second Secretary Lakshmi Swaminathan, who is working in my office, to prepare a detailed chart of the 2014 elections. Lakshmi has shown a propensity and willingness to spend hours ferreting out details from historical records. It is time to put her skills to good use and discern any trends that can come in handy this election.

What Lakshmi churns out, with the help of her contacts in the UN library, is fascinating. The voting records indicate that despite never being in the lead during over fourteen rounds in the Security Council, the Jamaican candidate, Patrick Lipton Robinson, had translated his consistent lead in the General Assembly into victory over the Argentine candidate, Susana Myrta Ruiz Cerutti, in the fifteenth round.[2]

This is a new pathway. I suggest that Lakshmi, along with her better half, Swaminathan, who also is an attache in our mission, prepare a detailed PowerPoint presentation for all of us to pore over and analyse. But before that, we need to be sure if this was a one-off situation or not. Was it a trend that we could validate with other past precedents? More work needs to be done.

As Lakshmi is already handling loads of other work, we look around for someone to entrust with this deep dive into the history of ICJ elections. Lakshmi suggests that young Zeeshan could perhaps be asked to do this onerous job. An engineering graduate who chose to follow his passion at Columbia University as a student of International Affairs, Mohammed Zeeshan is interning as a researcher/consultant with the mission during the course of the summer. He is keen, enthusiastic and intellectually eager to take on the task. Unencumbered by other work, he delves into the history of ICJ elections, carefully studying the past and providing raw details we can examine to discern trends that may help us strategize.

So copious is the data churned out by him that it takes the Swaminathan duo over a fortnight of struggle to bring coherence to it and dumb it down for our consumption. As we go through the PowerPoint presentation during one of our weekly evening meetings, we understand the complicated meaning of the trend lines of past elections.

The outcome of the 2014 elections is similar to the outcome of the 2011 elections, when Uganda's Judge Julia Sebutinde unseated Judge Abdul Koroma of Sierra Leone in the ninth round, despite never once leading against him in the Security Council. In 2011, as in 2014, the candidate who led in a direct contest in the General Assembly ultimately prevailed over the candidate who had a lead in the Security Council.

Zeeshan's research, as collated and presented by Lakshmi, highlights many other such instances. In 1990, Judge Raymond Ranjeva of Madagascar outlasted Judge Cheikh Tidiane Sy of Senegal despite trailing in the first two of three ballots in the Security Council. Similarly, in 1993, Judge Koroma of Sierra Leone defeated another African contender, Judge José Luís Jesus of Cape Verde; despite never getting an absolute majority in the Security Council in two rounds, he extended his lead in the General Assembly to a wide margin.

Discussing the various ICJ elections of the past over several hours that evening enhances our collective understanding of the nuances of ICJ elections. It makes us realize that in this complex election process, our Achilles heel of not gaining large support amongst the fifteen Security Council members on account of a late start need not sink us entirely so long as we ramp up support in the General Assembly. In most multi-seat contests, many of the seats are settled early and then direct contests ensue between the remaining candidates for the last seat. In such contests, the dynamics change completely. It is not about past commitments or slender leads in the Security Council. It is candidates who dominate the balloting in the larger General Assembly who are invariably triumphant, irrespective of how they fare amongst the fifteen members of the Security Council.

During such discussions, it is our practice to also have a Red Team, which takes a contrarian view and asks hostile questions. This time, Red Team is headed by Counsellor Mayank Joshi—a diplomat who has served two years at the UN, the longest period amongst all of us—who teams up with First Secretary Paulomi Tripathi, recently requisitioned for the election. Together, they launch a fusillade of queries.

'It is true that in theory there is no geographical allocation of the seats. But in reality, the seat being vacated by a judge has, as per convention, invariably been won by a judge from the same region,' they argue. 'There is a "de facto" geographical distribution of seats whatever may be the "de jure" position,' says Paulomi vociferously. Mayank voices the fear that since both Judge Bhandari and Nawaf Salam of Lebanon are from the Asia-Pacific region, in real terms the race will result in the two dividing the 193 votes in the General Assembly and fifteen votes in the Security Council amongst them as the members are likely to see them as vying for the same seat. On the other hand, they say, 'The number of candidates from other regions is equal to the number of judges completing the term from that region. They will have the full support of their region and will sail through easily.' The contention of the duo is that a multi-cornered election for multiple seats would in effect be a direct contest between the two candidates from the Asia-Pacific.

'It is entirely correct that a judge from one region has been succeeded by another from the same region. However, there are numerous instances during past ICJ elections where two candidates from the same region have together amassed between 200–250 votes in the General Assembly and seventeen to nineteen votes in the Security Council, when only one judge was retiring from the region,' responds Lakshmi. She provides several instances of candidates from the same region garnering more than 40 per cent in excess of the 193 votes in the General Assembly and 25 per cent more than the fifteen votes in the Security Council. 'It clearly indicates that UN members are not voting for candidates only along lines of regional distribution of seats,' is her conclusion.

'The dynamics of multi-seat contests are different from direct contests is what the data is pointing to,' says Tanmaya, citing the same examples. 'It is not unusual for the candidates from the same region to garner more votes than what would be the maximum possible in a direct contest, or if the votes were as per regional allocation of seats,' is his contention. He points out that in 2014, the Latin American and Caribbean duo of Jamaica's Patrick Robinson and Argentina's Susana Ruiz Cerutti cumulatively notched up more than 200 votes in each of the seven rounds that they contested along with six others, although only one of the five retiring judges was from that regional group. 'If this was a direct contest between the two for a single seat, the cumulative total of the two would not have exceeded 193 in the General Assembly and fifteen in the Security Council,' he explains. Multi-cornered elections for multiple seats provide opportunities for strong candidates to reach beyond regional groups to make up for shortcomings on other counts. We conclude that the data indicates that there are possibilities that could and need to be pursued by expanding our canvas and not projecting our candidate as one from the Asia-Pacific region alone.

In multilateral diplomacy, a proper intellectual understanding of a situation is as much an integral part of planning as is operational nimbleness. Perhaps, even more, in terms of mental preparation. This experience of scanning big data to look for a path forward in a difficult situation can stand all of us in good stead as we plug ahead at the UN. That evening, many of us leave the red stone structure of our mission in New York long past our usual departure time, but with a second wind garnered from a better understanding of history.

Yet, as each of us pursues interlocutors with greater intensity, the opportunities we had lost by delaying the announcement of Judge Bhandari's candidature are surfacing in starker detail. The difficulty of breaking out of the 'late entrant' label accounts for one less competitor by mid-August. About two months after Zambia announced the candidature of Chaloka Beyani, he withdraws.[3] It is apparent to us too that the spate of 'too late' responses needs to be addressed by us too. In some cases, they are genuine. In other instances, it is a way to ward off our persistent requests.

Bolivia's affable Ambassador Sacha Sergio Llorenti Soliz, who is serving on the Security Council, confides in me that between April and May his election officer had repeatedly sought confirmation from his Indian counterpart regarding whether India had a candidate for the ICJ; they always supported India and had wanted to be certain before they decided. 'Every time, your colleagues assured my diplomat that this was not on the table. Hence, we decided from available candidates. You have now put us in a predicament.' It is harsh, but true.

A French diplomat tells one of my colleagues that we had agreed to reciprocal arrangements between the French candidate for the ICJ and the Indian ITLOS candidate last year. 'By short-sightedly pursuing a single vote for June 2017, you lost two of ours in 2017,' she says. Again, factually correct, but that is not the full picture.

Buoyed by the information we have gleaned from the brainstorming, we start making the pitch that each delegation has five votes to cast. There are no provisions of regional quotas in the Statute of the ICJ. Instead, it provides for representation of the main forms of civilization and of the principal legal systems of the world. The impeccable judicial credentials of Judge Bhandari and India's judicial traditions are deserving of one of the five votes on all these counts.

Basically, our effort is to emphasize that while we are late, and therefore Judge Bhandari may not perhaps figure as one of the top few choices, India's credentials are such that it deserves to be at least one of the five choices. This approach provides more space for each country to consider the 'late entrant', rather than to shut him out completely. It enables us to work diplomatically with each of them.

Since we have exhausted most options of reciprocal tie-ups in New York, Joint Secretary Manish Chauhan at our headquarters is the go-to person to look at other options available globally— in what can be considered as potential trade-offs. Responding to my plea he says, 'Every forthcoming international election is fair game.' He narrates the requests that are being made as we push the pedal on Judge Bhandari's candidature. Elections to various global bodies, including the United Nations Educational, Scientific and Cultural Organization (UNESCO) in Paris, the World Customs Organization (WCO) in Brussels, the International Telecommunications Union (ITU) in Geneva, and the International Atomic Energy Agency (IAEA) in Vienna, are being leveraged by Manish and his team to assiduously build up support for Judge Bhandari—one vote at a time. Thanks to the diligence of our colleagues in Delhi and the persistent efforts of very many Indian diplomats in missions across the globe, the number of commitments for Judge Bhandari keeps rising steadily.

Our point person in Delhi, Vinod Jacob, with the help of the cloud computing skills of a young foreign service officer, Yatin Patil, conjures up an elaborate chart to track the responses of each of the 192 other members. Painstakingly data mining the multitude of responses received from New York, as well as data points provided by all our diplomatic outposts globally, they piece together the numbers and assess Judge Bhandari's support to be about eighty-five, including six Security Council members. Still well below the required 'absolute' majority in either body, the numbers are at least within striking range.

Come September, the primary interest of all delegations in New York is to ensure the successful participation of each of their delegations at the marquee event of the year, Leaders Week. Annually, more than a hundred kings and queens, presidents and prime ministers descend on New York. The arrangements for their stay, movement and engagements need so much attention that logistics is the principal preoccupation, indeed obsession, of UN diplomats. Hotel room bookings, motorcade movements, meeting locations and media coverage take centre stage. Everything else takes a back seat.

While much of the focus is on public diplomacy, the availability of so many senior dignitaries at one location also provides opportunities for quiet diplomacy. Leaders Week is an unparalleled opportunity for countries like ours to engage those with whom we may not have regular high-level interaction. After all, we do not even have embassies in more than a third of UN member states—to be precise, in seventy-five states. Much of such engagement does not attract attention and goes unreported. The media is usually focused on our ties with, at best, two dozen countries. The rest may not matter to them but are important for our multilateral diplomacy.

At the Leaders Week of the 72nd session, our goal is to engage with as many of the seventy-five as possible so as to ensure that we are able to get their commitments. External Affairs Minister Sushma Swaraj understands the critical importance of this opportunity. She agrees that her meetings should be largely targeted towards those we had no other opportunities to engage with in recent months at a political level. She also requests that Minister of State M.J. Akbar join her during the week to broaden our engagement levels and maximize, to the extent possible, the avenues for quiet diplomacy amidst the razzmatazz of Leaders Week. This is not unusual. The UK has its prime minister and more than half a dozen ministers attending various events and meetings, in a bid to show their activism at the UN.

Our media focuses on the usual India–Pakistan diatribes during the General Debate by the leaders of the respective delegations, Prime Minister Shahid Khaqan Abbasi[4] and External Affairs Minister Sushma Swaraj.[5] Additionally, their appetite is whetted by First Secretary Eenam Gambhir terming Pakistan as 'Terroristan' in her response to the Pakistani leader's statement.[6] And then First Secretary Paulomi Tripathi, in her UN debut, tearing apart the false narrative projected by the Pakistani Permanent Representative Ambassador Maleeha Lodhi, who displays a picture of a Palestinian girl and seeks to pass her off as a Kashmiri.[7] These are what constitute the main themes of our participation during Leaders Week in 2017 as transmitted by our media to those who follow India's multilateral engagements at the UN that year.

However, for us in the diplomatic establishment, the importance of the week goes beyond the public diplomacy postures. By the end of September, we are able to meet the minimum threshold for an absolute majority at the forthcoming ICJ elections on account of the whirlwind meetings that our ministers have had with many of their counterparts. We now have a month left to further consolidate, beyond the low bar that we have managed to surmount on account of the last three months of concerted efforts.

5

We Have Done Well,
So Have the Others

Sunday, 1 October – Wednesday, 8 November 2017

THE UN IS viewed, not without sufficient reason, as functioning in a bubble. The nearly 10,000 diplomats engaged in an array of activities in New York come with distinctive baggage from each of their different backgrounds. However, their collective engagements at the UN engender a sense of commonality that tends to bind them together and overshadow the diversity of their interests. The focused pursuit of national goals, in an atmosphere where a multiplicity of activities are underway simultaneously, is an acquired skill. It stems from a process of acculturation, which is usually not easy, especially for diplomats from countries not on the Security Council. They have to navigate by themselves across a broad swathe of items, think on their feet, find niches where they matter and contribute in significant ways to global good, even while pursuing their own pet themes.

Also, working effectively in the numerous processes requires forming effective partnerships. The UN is no place for lone rangers. That is the prerogative of diplomats from the permanent member states of the Security Council (P-5), whose privileged perches provide immense opportunities for leveraging to meet their goals. The rest of us learn to work in innovative ways to be effective in this vast, stratified universe. Hence, many countries place a premium on longer tenures and repeated multilateral postings for their diplomats so that skill sets, once acquired, can be honed and used for national advantage. Given the number of officers in the Indian Foreign Service and the matrix that is used to provide for equity in postings, it is rare for any officer to be deputed more than once to a multilateral organization for a three-year period before gaining an ambassadorial rank of Permanent Representative or Deputy Permanent Representative.

Usually, we try to make up for this lack of long experience with more effective coordination and greater sharing of information. Clarity amongst all colleagues at the mission, one of our primary goals, is critical to our effectiveness. It enables each of us to chalk out pathways, while always being aware of our broader UN environment. The derisively nicknamed 'prayer' meeting is an integral component of my own effort at fostering greater cohesiveness. Every day, we usually begin at 9.15 a.m. when all diplomats troop into my office for a 'tour de table'. It lasts no longer than twenty to thirty minutes. Each diplomat mentions in a minute or two any issue of importance that is on the platter, or an outcome that others will find useful. This provides all of us a quick understanding of the major issues for the day and the lie of the land on each of them. Where more detailed discussions or instructions are required, the diplomats concerned stay back and follow up with Tanmaya and me after the meeting. Come hail or snow, these meetings are invariably the first order of business. If I am busy elsewhere at another early-morning event, Tanmaya holds the meeting in my room so that in case I am back early I can join in too. Since most young diplomats stay on the premises, the onus is on Tanmaya and me, who stay outside, to be on time. Happily, both of us are of the punctual variety.

The discipline of updating ourselves regularly at the start of the day and constantly thereafter is coming in handy in ways that we did not envisage when we began this process in 2016. However, at times such as now when stress levels rise, it needs to be calibrated by not being too forceful. Sometimes, colleagues are unhappy at being pushed beyond their comfort zones. A young diplomat stays back after others leave and wants to speak to me alone following a testy period of questioning about her efforts during a morning meeting. 'I am not the sharpest knife in this kitchen, but today it was not my fault. It was just my turn,' she bursts out. It is a signal that I am, occasionally, being unreasonable. As we race against time to expand our support base ahead of the final denouement scheduled for early November, stress levels are increasing all around. Such feedback is useful. It ensures that in the quest to recalibrate our energies in directions we may not otherwise have addressed, there is a need to be considerate towards individual sensitivities too.

At a broader level, the key to getting a country's message across in the veritable babble of incoherence that the UN seems to be is as much a question of style as it is of substance. As part of a conscious effort at strategic messaging of our activism, we have over more than a year enhanced the intensity of our UN engagements across various issues. The International Day of Yoga has become a fixture in the UN calendar, and the activities associated with the celebrations attract a large number of UN diplomats and staff. The lighting up of lamps on the UN premises to mark the first observance of Diwali as a 'floating' holiday garnered huge interest. A.R. Rahman's concert at the General Assembly Hall to celebrate India's seventieth Independence Day was widely regarded as better in terms of production quality and audience interest than Beyoncé's earlier concert at the same venue.

More substantively, the India–UN Development Partnership for sustainable development, initiated in June 2017, generated enormous interest amongst several small island states and the least developed countries inside the UN bubble. We have ventured on this solo 'start-up' effort, drawing upon the success of the established India–Brazil–South Africa (IBSA) Fund.[1] To use the proper nomenclature, the IBSA Facility for Poverty and Hunger Alleviation was established in 2004 and operationalized through the Office of South–South Cooperation at the UN since 2006. It was a pioneering tripartite effort at South–South cooperation. Each of the three countries contributed $1 million annually and agreed to implement development projects primarily through UN agencies. The template was simple and was used over a decade to fund several small development projects in developing countries.

Buoyed by this success, over a decade later, we established in 2017 the India–UN Development Partnership Fund focused on the implementation of SDGs by leveraging the presence of the UN system in various small islands and developing countries.[2] The goal is to extend our outreach in countries where we do not have a diplomatic presence and are likely to find it difficult to support development projects directly.

The first project on climate early warning systems, in the Pacific states of Cook Islands, Federated States of Micronesia, Kiribati, Nauru, Republic of the Marshall Islands, Solomon

Islands and Tonga, was announced in June 2017.[3] The initiative is now generating huge interest amongst representatives of small states and various UN agencies as a possible new source for voluntary funding amidst the difficult financial situation they are facing. External Affairs Minister Sushma Swaraj, having quickly grasped its potential, has enhanced the first year's contribution from $1 million to $5 million during her visit to New York in September. She also announces humanitarian relief contributions to Hurricane Erma-hit Antigua and Barbuda, and Dominica.[4] The swiftness of using the assistance through the UN system is leading to a manifest growth of interest and enthusiasm for the Fund, especially among the more than thirty small island developing states which are a coherent group at the UN.

Ngedikes 'Olai' Uludong, the former military police woman and sprightly climate activist who is now serving as Palau's Permanent Representative to the UN, candidly tells me, 'The Fund marks the transition of India at the UN. You have moved from voicing declaratory support on development issues to providing concrete and tangible support for our development goals.' She is voicing a view that many others are echoing in different ways.

In the past, within the UN bubble, India was viewed as vocal in declaratory support of the development priorities of developing countries. States where we have no diplomatic presence are now seeing us as potential contributors to their specific development requirements. They are right. In the few months since the Fund was set up in 2017, it has a burgeoning portfolio of projects, and announcements of more commitments are indicated over the longer term.[5] In these early days, the immediate and welcome impact of some of the enthusiasm for the India–UN Development Fund is that it is also playing into support for our ICJ election effort.

The pattern of responses coming through from many developing countries indicates that rather than being merely part of a bubble, the UN missions are semi-permeable. Those we have strong bilateral ties with are forthright in affirming support, drawing attention to the strength of our relationship. In other cases, our support at the UN on issues of interest to them is important. For example, some states—especially from the Pacific and Caribbean—point out that the development initiatives we have undertaken through the IBSA Fund and the India–UN Development Partnership Fund reflect our concrete support for their national development goals at the UN.

All through the month of October, the numbers trickling in from various quarters indicate a growth of support for Judge Bhandari. This is primarily on account of support being confirmed by very many small states. They constitute the vast majority of UN members. By an authoritative count, states with a population of less than 10 million account for 110 of the 193 members of the UN. So, from a perspective, this was good going. However, several of the big states remain a matter of concern. As a corollary, our assessment of the tally in the Security Council is remaining static. It continues to hover just around the required majority of eight. For a variety of reasons, more are not forthcoming in support. Thus for us, there is no space for any slippage. We are repeatedly sounding the warning bells that this is placing us in a situation of extreme vulnerability. From New York our repeated plea to New Delhi is that this situation needs to be addressed by being taken up appropriately in capitals by our resident heads of mission and, where necessary, through special envoys sent from Delhi. However, the intensity of focus over the past three months is such that perhaps there is a belief that, like Oliver Twist, I always want 'some more'. It could also be that there is a feeling of fatigue and inertia setting in now since several efforts have been made, and the needle has scarcely moved. Going into the final stretch, this remains a problem that we have not been able to address fully.

The final days before any election are a blitz involving numerous receptions and meetings. Rumours of all sorts are afloat, and suggestions for last-minute adjustments keep coming in from all directions. First Secretary Mahesh Kumar, who keeps a close watch on the activities of the Arab Group, says he senses that hush-hush discussions are underway. 'Plans are afoot for "tactical" voting by Arab states only in support of their candidate—Nawaf Salam—to the exclusion of all others,' he crestfallenly reports one evening. Listening in, Election Officer Anjani Kumar is as nervous as a cat on a hot tin roof. He explains that small groups tend to work on their own, following the formality of voting as per solemn commitments in the initial round. Given the configuration of the six candidates who have put in so much effort, it is certain that all of them will get the required majority in the first round. All that the candidates require is about one-ninth of the total votes cast in each of the two bodies to get the required majority. Multiple rounds seem inevitable.

Part of my job is also to keep following up on clues that my young colleagues come up with, even if it means pestering other ambassadors repeatedly and listening to their set-piece responses. In this instance, Mahesh Kumar's concerns are worrisome. I make a round of calls to ascertain the situation. A friendly Arab ambassador sheepishly responds, 'Tactical support for the Arab candidates has been discussed and plans are afoot. It does not mean all will be on board, but some are already there.' These were the 'tricks of the trade' of those who have been in the bubble for long. Whatever may be the commitments made, those who are charged with deciding on the spot hold sway. It does not augur well for us if we do not do very well at the outset.

Meanwhile, like all other candidates, Judge Bhandari too is back in New York for the final phase. He is going through, again and again, with the sales pitch—wherever it is needed. He has honed his pitch, having made it for receptions held to promote his candidature in Delhi by Minister Swaraj and in The Hague by Ambassador Venu Rajamony. The initial reticence is now replaced by a willingness—indeed eagerness—to do more, but always within what he considers are boundaries of making his case as an objective jurist. Judge Bhandari's wife, who is accompanying him, is a reassuring presence keeping his spirits high as he is going through the chores of seeking votes in small groups and larger receptions.

Number crunching is a difficult task at UN elections. This is because different countries adopt different ways of signalling support. The easiest of course is to go by written support. But some states have the practice of never giving written support. Some others, as recent elections at the UN have indicated, tend to keep all happy by confirming to more candidates than the votes available to them. An apocryphal anecdote that usually does the rounds amongst UN diplomats relates to the election of the President of the General Assembly in 2016, when the two candidates in the fray together had written commitments from more than 220, when the total number of voters was 193. Notwithstanding the many perils and pitfalls of making calculations in such an environment, it is an essential task that has to be gone through in all elections.

Usually, the practice followed is to adopt a deflator based on past experiences. In our case, we inevitably reduce written commitments by 10 per cent and other assurances by 25 per cent. This is a conservative method, but it has worked in past elections, providing ballpark figures which were fairly close to our final tally.

Following the close of business at the UN late in the evening of 8 November, having taken into account all submissions made by Election Officer Anjani Kumar and from New Delhi as well as all capitals, I do the figures repeatedly. They work out to 148 in the General Assembly and nine in the Security Council. Accounting for any errors I may have made in being conservative, I put down a minimum of 150 and ten in my final assessment that is sent out that night.

Our numbers alone do not matter, as we have no clear idea of what the others are likely to get. Also, what will happen after the initial vote remains uncertain, since all the six candidates are sure to get more than the minimum required? Getting a high number in the first round does not guarantee success if the competition is close. Although those were different times, there is a historical precedent that we are not unaware of. In 1954, Judge Radhabinod Pal eventually lost to Pakistan's Sir Muhammad Zafrullah Khan despite pipping him in the first round in the General Assembly with thirty-two votes to his thirty. A second round was held, as none had got the 'absolute' majority of thirty-three from the sixty-four members entitled to vote, although only sixty-two were present. According to a little-known anecdote, fixing the date of the election on a Jewish religious holiday (on which the Israeli delegation that had decided to vote for Pal would not be present) effectively determined the issue against the Indian candidate.[6] In the second round, Khan secured thirty-three votes against Pal's twenty-nine.[7] Close votes generally tend to favour insiders, and Zafrullah Khan was one then. He was the Pakistani Permanent Representative at the UN, while Radhabinod Pal was a quintessential jurist.

—✕—

Thursday, 9 November 2017
New York

Most of us assemble, as usual, at 9.15 a.m. at the mission. We wish each other well. There is nothing to discuss. All leave for the UN to join those who were positioned there for logistical purposes ahead of the others. It usually takes us about ten minutes to get to the UN premises from our mission. We are all in place well before the scheduled start of 10 a.m. Since elections are to be held simultaneously, Tanmaya and First Secretary Sandeep Kumar are in the Security Council to follow its activities, and Legal Adviser Umasankar is there to assist them if necessary. The rest of us are positioned in the General Assembly Hall and are allocated different aisles so that we can move around to meet designated delegations. We know our roles; we have been through this before—only the stage this time is much larger, and the stakes much higher.

On entering the cavernous General Assembly Hall, what strikes me is that all the five judges seeking re-election are already there, seated in the gallery reserved for important visitors. Judge Bhandari and his fellow judges seem to share a good sense of camaraderie. It is nice to see all of them chatting animatedly. Nevertheless, they, like Nawaf, whom I greeted just outside the hall, are understandably nervous. Their teams are all around, making last-minute pleas. The delegates' desks present a different picture from past elections. In accordance with the recent decision of the General Assembly,[8] they are no longer strewn with gifts and large amounts of paper. All that is now allowed is a pamphlet on behalf of each of the six candidates. The hall is packed with a large number of delegates, as the election has drawn considerable interest.

Voting by secret ballot in the Security Council is usually a swift process as only fifteen delegations are seated along the horseshoe table. In the 193-member General Assembly, it is time-consuming, as it entails the distribution and collection of ballots by many 'tellers' chosen from different delegations that do not have candidates contesting, and then there is counting and recounting to ensure there are no errors. The first round with six candidates in the fray takes a long time, nearly ninety minutes. Although the Security Council process is over in less than thirty minutes, the results are announced together and in a coordinated manner. It provides time for diplomats, like me, who do not have seats on the Security Council to cast our votes in the General Assembly Hall and then go across to the Security Council Chamber, to talk to colleagues (in my case, at times Tanmaya and Sandeep) and seek their assessment. It also enables me to meet Security Council delegates from other countries and seek reassurances of their support ahead of the next round.

Both Tanmaya and I are at our seats, sitting side by side at the India desk in the General Assembly Hall, when Miroslav Lajčák (foreign minister of the Slovak Republic, who has taken leave of absence for the year to function full time as the President of the UN General Assembly) announces that all 193 members have voted. Simultaneously, Sandeep, who is in the Security Council, informs us that the results are being announced there too. The results, as announced by President Lajčák in the General Assembly and by President Cardi (Italy) in the Security Council, are as follows:

Candidate	COUNTRY	ROUND 1	
		SC	GA
Antonio Augusto Cancado Trindade	BRAZIL	11	153
Ronny Abraham	FRANCE	15	165
Dalveer Bhandari	INDIA	11	149
Nawaf Salaam	LEBANON	11	148
Abdulqawi Ahmed Yusuf	SOMALIA	12	144
Christopher Greenwood	UK	14	147
TOTAL VOTES CAST		74*	906*
TOTAL VOTES AVAILABLE		75**	905**

* Total votes cast: 74 in the Security Council by 15 members and 906 in the General Assembly by 193 members. Not all use all the votes available.
** Total votes available: 75 as all 15 members were present and had 5 votes in the Security Council, and 965 in the General Assembly as all 193 members were present and had 5 votes each available to cast.

Vinod Jacob had set up, in July, an online forum for interaction consisting of all key decision makers in the Ministry of External Affairs and our mission. It had not been used much earlier as speed was not of the essence then. It now comes in handy as the results are being transmitted to all simultaneously. In a trice, it is transformed into a key platform for sharing information. Henceforth, it is the new go-to internal tool that is instrumental in getting all of us on the same page on so many small but important facets of the election process and many other matters. Of necessity, we have moved to a new normal in our internal practices, sharing information quickly and engaging with each other in real-time like never before.

Even as I transmit the results, I can hear my colleagues sitting behind me heave a collective sigh of relief. The votes we poll are in keeping with our painstakingly assessed numbers. In the General Assembly, we get one vote less and, in the Security Council, one more than what we had anticipated. Everyone scored well above the thresholds of the 'absolute' majority of ninety-seven in the General Assembly and eight in the Security Council. There are no winners, nor are there any losers. All remain in the fray. None has fallen below any of the required thresholds. This is not a simple election where winning is determined by getting to be in the top five vote getters. It is an election where someone has to lose in both fora by not getting the 'absolute' majority. We have done well, so have all the others.

6

What Is Happening?

Thursday, 9 November 2017
New York

E VEN AS THE next round of voting is being announced, words I had often heard colleagues say flash through my mind: 'All bets are off after the first round.' It is a disconcerting and an extremely worrisome thought. We are entering uncharted territory. Tanmaya, sitting beside me, seems to read my thoughts.

'You are worried?' he whispers so that others do not pick it up.

'I think we are in trouble. The vote is too close. If the past is any indication, it will go down from now on,' I respond with distinct unease.

There is nothing we can do immediately as the next round of balloting is to follow quickly. Tanmaya goes back to the Security Council, while I try to cover up my nervousness and cheer my other colleagues for the good results. Judge Bhandari is in the top half of the candidates in the General Assembly, and the number of votes he secures in the Council has exceeded what we anticipated. Encouraged, my colleagues go about pursuing as many of their designated interlocutors as is possible in the few minutes they have.

Once the voting is over and the counting is underway, a colleague from an African state who has been at the UN for more than five years comes over and conveys his concern. 'Judge Yusuf, the African candidate, is polling the lowest in the General Assembly. This is not fair. We are watching. This round's results will determine whether we switch tactics,' he ends ominously without clarifying what 'switching tactics' means. With the counting system now streamlined, the results of the second round come in rapidly.[1]

Candidate	COUNTRY	Round 1		Round 2	
		SC	GA	SC	GA
Antonio Augusto Cancado Trindade	BRAZIL	11	153	11	150
Ronny Abraham	FRANCE	15	165	15	159
Dalveer Bhandari	INDIA	11	149	10	141
Nawaf Salaam	LEBANON	11	148	11	150
Abdulqawi Ahmed Yusuf	SOMALIA	12	144	12	141
Christopher Greenwood	UK	14	147	14	137
TOTAL VOTES CAST		74	906	73	878
TOTAL VOTES AVAILABLE		75	965	75	965

All six candidates again poll in excess of the required majority of ninety-seven in the General Assembly and eight in the

Security Council. It means another vote is to follow. However, there are some visible trends. Although, as in the first round, all 193 members are present and voting, the total votes polled fall by twenty-eight in the General Assembly and by one in the Security Council. While it is our vote that is reduced by one in the Council, in the General Assembly, votes polled by five of the six candidates are lower. Only Nawaf Salam's vote count has increased in the General Assembly; the votes of all the rest are lower than in the previous round. The consummate insider seems to be at work.

Tanmaya and Sandeep at the Security Council text that while they are not certain who could have abstained and not voted for us in the second round, they mention that there seems to have been a change in the case of one member of the Council. An ambassador who had voted in the first round left soon after on account of travel plans and instead another delegate from the same country is now voting.

'The shift in our vote count can be on account of that change of personnel,' is Sandeep's belief, as there are no other reasons for the reduction in our tally. The bonus vote that we had not accounted for in our calculations prior to the initial vote is now no longer there.

More worrisome is the decline of eight votes in the General Assembly. A host of theories rush to my mind. However, with no luxury of time to think through and understand the implications—the third round of voting is scheduled to begin as soon as the results of the second round are announced—I brush aside all thoughts, for the time being, and sit down to vote again.

The interval between the vote and the announcement of results is usually about half an hour. This is the best time to gain insights from other diplomats to learn about their assessments of the fluctuations in votes.

'What is happening?' I probe Canadian ambassador Marc-André Blanchard. He is a lawyer-turned-diplomat. His passion for multilateralism made him move from the private sector to the UN. His bilingual abilities always provide perceptive insights into the Francophone world. He seems to have sized up the situation well. 'Group dynamics' are at play, he says. 'Some are only voting for their preferred candidate and not for anyone else,' is his succinct summation. Although each state can vote for five candidates, by voting only for a single candidate some small groups are boosting the chances of their preferred candidate, is his analysis. 'The total vote count will fall further,' he adds. 'Others will quickly join this game. Candidates with strong "group affiliations" will do better than those who don't have such affiliations,' he concludes.

The outcome of the third round of voting lends support to Ambassador Blanchard's assessment. In fact, he is in some ways extremely prescient. While the number of members present and voting remains the full house of 193 in the General Assembly, the total votes cast drop by more than 100. From the tally of 878 in the second round, they now total 781 in the third round. In comparison, with 906 cast in the first round, the reduction is 125 votes. Even in the Security Council, only sixty-six votes are cast, as against seventy-three in the second round and seventy-four in the first round. After the initial vote, more than 10 per cent votes are not cast in both bodies.

If in the second round the tally of only one candidate had not declined in the General Assembly, it is again so in the third round. But this time it is another candidate—Judge Yusuf of Somalia. He retains his tally of 141 votes, while the votes of all the other candidates dip. As was the indication, some African friends had decided to change tactics too, following others. All candidates, except for Judge Yusuf, poll between fourteen and twenty-eight votes less in the third round than they had garnered in the second round in the General Assembly.[2]

In the Security Council too, all candidates—except for France's Judge Ronny Abraham—poll lower than in the previous round. Brazil's Judge Trindade drops three votes and is precipitously on eight votes. All the other candidates drop one vote each. Judge Bhandari polls nine votes.

Candidate	COUNTRY	Round 1		Round 2		Round 3	
		SC	GA	SC	GA	SC	GA
Antonio Augusto Cancado Trindade	BRAZIL	11	153	11	150	8	131
Ronny Abraham	FRANCE	15	165	15	159	15	144
Dalveer Bhandari	INDIA	11	149	10	141	9	120
Nawaf Salam	LEBANON	11	148	11	150	10	136
Abdulqawi Ahmed Yusuf	SOMALIA	12	144	12	141	11	141
Christopher Greenwood	UK	14	147	14	137	13	109

TOTAL VOTES CAST		74	906	73	878	66	781
TOTAL VOTES AVAILABLE		75	965	75	965	75	965

There is plenty of food for thought and concern as we set about digesting the implications of the outcome of the last round during the adjournment for lunch. As we come out of the General Assembly Hall, I come across Ambassador Mauro Vieira of Brazil, who had come over to the UN after having served as the foreign minister. He asks me the question that I had gone about asking others, 'What is happening?'

I tell him about the talk I had heard of 'group dynamics'. He is worried that the Brazilian judge's vote in the Security Council has fallen to eight and he can't afford any more of a decrease.

⎯⎯⎯ ⦿⦿⦿ ⎯⎯⎯

At the UN, according to old-timers, the best place to gather information is to saunter across the corridor from the General Assembly Hall to the Security Council chambers. They say: it is likely you will come across several other colleagues on the way and can seek their counsel. This afternoon, I take that advice even as others are leaving for lunch. I come across a colleague from Africa beaming at me. He is happy with the change in fortunes in the last round. Judge Yusuf has clambered to the top half of candidates in the General Assembly. When I remind him of his commitment to support Judge Bhandari, he smiles and says, 'No hard feelings. We have to first feather our own nest before helping others.'

A little further ahead, I meet an Arab ambassador I have known for many years as we had served together as young diplomats at the UN in the 1990s. I seek reassurance of support for Judge Bhandari. He takes me aside and steers me towards the huge glass panes that overlook the patches of grass between the General Assembly and the Secretariat buildings. Once we have moved away from the stream of diplomats rushing to and fro along the corridor, he mutters, 'I fulfilled my commitment in the first round. Now, we are only for the two Arab candidates from Lebanon and Somalia.'

As I reach the Council chambers, I run into the Bolivian ambassador, Sacha Llorenti, who, as a member of the Council, had stayed back to have some discussions and was heading for lunch. Over the last few months, we have engaged on several occasions, and I have grown to respect his very nuanced and thoughtful views. As we exchange notes, he explains that 'group loyalties' are now 'primary'. He says, 'I am surprised by this turn of events, but as a strong votary of Latin interests, I am keen to ensure that the Brazilian judge doesn't lose any more votes in the Council.' To the exclusion of all else, it seems he is working with others to ensure this. Like the others, he too does not provide reassurance of support in a fluid situation.

'Group dynamics' are clearly in full play. Ambassador Blanchard, a disinterested observer, has discerned the interplay remarkably astutely. Others are confirming it. France has the support of the Francophonie group and, along with the UK, is part of the club of the Permanent Five. Both have five votes sewn up in the Council in all circumstances as part of the unwritten understanding that all permanent members vote for each other. The Somali candidate has the solid support of the African group, and also belongs to the Arab group; the Lebanese candidate has Arab, Francophonie and OIC support, and personal equities built over years. The Brazilian candidate has the Latin group working for him at full throttle. There is only one candidate who lacks support from a cohesive group— Judge Bhandari.

Digesting all this leaves me with no appetite for lunch. If 'group dynamics' play out, we have no group of whose consistent support we can be certain. More importantly, we cannot play this game to the detriment of others as they were playing to their benefit. Since we are disproportionately dependent on the support of groups that have membership from developing countries, such as Africa and the Arabs, we are impacted much more than those who are not dependent on such support. Also, it is difficult to discern who amongst the various groups are only voting for 'their' candidate/candidates. It is not entire groups that are resorting to 'tactical voting'. All it requires is a small core of the various groups to use such tactics to have a disproportionate impact on the outcome. For example, the reduction of 100 votes in the General Assembly can easily be the handiwork of twenty-five delegates. The reduction of eight votes in the Security Council can be on account of just two representatives.

The notion of 'group loyalty' usually means that candidates supported by certain groups would have the support of their members. However, what is playing out now is not limited to voting for a candidate from the group to which a state belongs. It has metamorphosed into the tactics of a few from some groups voting only for their favoured candidate and not using their entire tally of available votes. This means that an 'us and the rest' approach is being adopted by some.

I call Tanmaya and ask him and Sandeep to meet as many Security Council members as possible during the lunch to seek reassurance of support. For my part, I also contact six Security Council ambassadors who are available. Each reassures us of the support that they had conveyed previously. For their part, Tanmaya and Sandeep are able to contact all their interlocutors. They report that most, including those we are certain will not vote for us, assure that they will indeed vote for us. Clearly, they are not showing their cards in a difficult situation. As diplomats, we have to grin and bear with such assurances even when we know some are not going to materialize. While we are upset about the twenty-nine-vote drop in Judge Bhandari's tally between the first and the third rounds of voting in the General Assembly, the more immediate danger is the Security Council. While Brazil is one short of falling below the required majority in the Security Council, we are not far behind and are two votes short of falling below the same majority. Without any group support, we are particularly susceptible in the Security Council in the manoeuvring of 'group loyalties'.

7

A Contest by Chance,
Not Choice

Thursday, 9 November 2017
New York

MULTILATERAL DIPLOMACY TENDS to teach its practitioners a range of life lessons—some good, some bad, and some ugly—sometimes, all in the space of a day. Engaging with the same set of interlocutors on a variety of issues ensures that you learn to take the good with the not-so-good in your stride. This seems to be one such day of running into rough patches with some colleagues and trying to figure out ways to make things go your way with others.

As we troop back into the General Assembly Hall after the lunch recess, a senior delegate from an important Asian state approaches me and hands over an envelope, whispering, 'You won't be unhappy with the contents.' It has a note indicating that previously they were unable to vote for us due to prior commitments. Those commitments have been fulfilled. Hence, they are committing to support Judge Bhandari during the rest of the election. I thank the delegate for their thoughtfulness and express our gratitude for their responsiveness in difficult circumstances.

The change comes as a pleasant surprise. It is a vote that we had pursued for long but had been repeatedly told that we were late; they had committed elsewhere. A few days prior to the election, there were hints given to our diplomats in their capital that they would perhaps be looking for a way out. There was no corroboration in New York. Thus, we had given up on that vote. Now, out of the blue, the afternoon has begun on a good note. Counsellor Anjani Kumar immediately collects the envelope from me with a big smile. However, the thought occurs to me that while we may have gained one vote in the General Assembly, it could well be that others may be swinging the other way—away from us—on the same basis that their commitments to us had been fulfilled. Signs that the situation is evolving, the rules are changing, and the tide too can change, seem to be all around.

The voting and counting following the lunch break takes long. Or so it seems. Tanmaya comes over from the Security Council to say that there is a lot of to and fro and hushed talk amongst the 'tellers'—delegates charged with the counting of votes. However, the result is being tightly held even as the General Assembly results are on the verge of announcement. Immediately afterwards, Sandeep, who is stationed in the Council chambers, calls to say that the President of the Council has announced that 'the voting in the Council was conclusive'. However, since the voting in the General Assembly was not 'conclusive', the Council will have to wait before announcing the full results in the Council and the General Assembly.

In other words, he was signalling that one of the six candidates had not been able to get 'absolute' majority in the Security Council, whereas that was not the case in the General Assembly. In accordance with the rules, the 'conclusive' results cannot be announced until the voting in the General Assembly too reaches a similar conclusion. Both Judge Bhandari and Judge

Candidate	COUNTRY	Round 1		Round 2		Round 3		Round 4	
		SC	GA	SC	GA	SC	GA	SC	GA
Antonio Augusto Cancado Trindade	BRAZIL	11	153	11	150	8	131	10	131
Ronny Abraham	FRANCE	15	165	15	159	15	144	15	137
Dalveer Bhandari	INDIA	11	149	10	141	9	120	7	121
Nawaf Salaam	LEBANON	11	148	11	150	10	136	12	136
Abdulqawi Ahmed Yusuf	SOMALIA	12	144	12	141	11	141	10	136
Christopher Greenwood	UK	14	147	14	137	13	109	12	102
TOTAL VOTES CAST		74	906	73	878	66	781	66	763
TOTAL VOTES AVAILABLE		75	965	75	965	75	965	75	960

Trindade, sitting together in the General Assembly gallery, are perceptibly anxious as I go over to explain the situation to them. While both are well above the required majority in the General Assembly, in the Security Council both were vulnerable; it could only be one of them who may have slipped further. Yet, as good friends, they are offering support to each other.

The results of the fourth round of the voting in General Assembly are as follows:[1]

The haemorrhaging of votes in the General Assembly has slowed down. While the total votes decline by a further eighteen, it is the lowest decline all day. Three candidates retain their votes—Judge Bhandari actually gains a vote, while Nawaf Salam and Judge Trindade poll the same as in the last round. The 'group dynamics' are still in play, but we have stabilized at where we were earlier in the day. Others continue to be impacted in the General Assembly. Even though the President of the Council has, in accordance with the procedures governing the election, informed the President of the General Assembly of the outcome of the 'conclusive' voting in the Council, the rest of us are not aware of it as we sit down for another round of balloting in the General Assembly. This maintains the sanctity of the separate processes and ensures that an outcome in one body does not adversely impact the process in the other body. However, at the back of our minds there is the concern that Judge Bhandari may have fallen short of the required majority in the Council.

If the time between the vote and the announcement of results felt long the last time, it now seems even longer. The votes are being recounted to ensure that the final tally is correct. It is a sign that the General Assembly too is reaching a conclusion. In simultaneous statements, the presidents of the General Assembly and the Security Council announce that as a result of the independent voting in the General Assembly and in the Security Council, four candidates have obtained an absolute majority in both bodies: Ronny Abraham, Antônio Augusto Cançado Trindade, Nawaf Salam and Abdulqawi Ahmed Yusuf. They are now, therefore, duly elected members of the International Court of Justice to serve for a nine-year term commencing on 6 February 2018. What is left unsaid is that Judge Dalveer Bhandari has fallen short of the absolute majority required in the Security Council, but Judge Christopher Greenwood of the UK too has similarly polled below the absolute majority required in the General Assembly.[2]

A huge collective gasp goes up in the General Assembly, as all of us present seek to absorb the enormity of the outcome. For the first time in its history, two incumbent judges of the ICJ have stumbled into an electoral contest and are now going to face each other. It is a contest from which only one can emerge victorious. Whatever the outcome, it is one for the history books.

Our legal adviser, Umasankar, anticipating that it may be useful to recollect Judge Christopher Greenwood's background, helpfully scribbles out a paragraph and slips it to me. It reads as follows: 'Born in 1955, the UK's candidate is seven years younger than Judge Bhandari. However, he is senior to Judge Bhandari on the ICJ, having joined in February 2009 following his election in November 2008. Judge Bhandari was elected in April 2012. When he was elected in 2008, Judge Greenwood had out-polled Judge Ronny Abraham of France, who has just been re-elected. As a student, Greenwood was the President of the Cambridge Union. Prior to his joining the ICJ, Greenwood was a professor of International Law at the London School of Economics. He has appeared as a counsel before the ICJ and other tribunals. He was knighted in 2009.'

Then, even as I am poring over the note to decipher his scrawl, he comes over and whispers, 'There are some controversies associated with him, I will let you know later.'

At this stage, my mind is wandering elsewhere. The realization that what we have always feared has happened is sinking in. Our shortcomings in the Security Council have indeed proved to be our undoing. However, luckily for us, the announcement of a further vote restricted to the two candidates—Judge Greenwood and Judge Bhandari—means that we have no time to absorb the shock, or even assess the final numbers in the Security Council or the possible shifts that may have caused the outcome. If this were not the case, we may have perhaps gone in search of a scapegoat, which as former US President Dwight Eisenhower said is 'the easiest of all hunting expeditions' and would certainly have been extremely diversionary.

Just as we didn't have the time to regroup, or to even seek support in the changed circumstances, all the others also have no advance knowledge that they will be required to make a choice—for which they are unprepared. None has envisaged that the final contest and choice they need to make will be between Judge Bhandari and Judge Greenwood, two sitting judges of the ICJ from different regions. They are now required to choose in a contest that has come to happen by chance, not by choice. They don't have advance instructions. Very few can get instructions from their capitals. We too

Candidate	COUNTRY	Round 1		Round 2		Round 3		Round 4		Round 5	
		SC	GA	SC	GA	SC	GA	SC	GA	SC	GA
Antonio Augusto Cancado Trindade	BRAZIL	11	153	11	150	8	131	10	131	-	127
Ronny Abraham	FRANCE	15	165	15	159	15	144	15	137	-	139
Dalveer Bhandari	INDIA	11	149	10	141	9	120	07	121	-	118
Nawaf Salaam	LEBANON	11	148	11	150	10	136	12	136	-	135
Abdulqawi Ahmed Yusuf	SOMALIA	12	144	12	141	11	141	10	136	-	137
Christopher Greenwood	UK	14	147	14	137	13	109	12	102	-	96
TOTAL VOTES CAST		74	906	73	878	66	781	66	763		752
TOTAL VOTES AVAILABLE		75	965	75	965	75	965	75	960		960

103

cannot seek support from Delhi in any way. The outcome will be, by and large, what is the unvarnished, natural disposition of UN members in New York.

In such a direct contest, the choice is always binary and clear. The scope for other actors to play their tactical games of only using a limited number of votes from a large number available is diminished. With only a single vote, each member has a clear choice to make—Judge Bhandari (India) or Judge Greenwood (UK). There is also no time to make a detailed assessment of the individual profiles and compare and contrast them as individuals. In most cases, it is a matter of the choice of the country.

If history is a guiding factor, then it will be the UK's Judge Greenwood. Every permanent member usually has a judge on the court. The only exception was in 1967–85, when there was no Chinese judge on the ICJ bench. However, it was on account of the special position of China in that period and because no Chinese candidate had contested. The beginning of this period was one when the Republic of China had occupied the Chinese seat at the UN. At the end of 1966, when the eighty-year-old incumbent Judge Wellington Koo (then Vice President of the ICJ) of China was retiring, no Chinese candidate was fielded. Even after the People's Republic of China took over representation at the UN, it did not nominate a candidate until 1984. Then finally Judge Zhengyu Ni was nominated and won.[3] He was the first judge of the ICJ from the People's Republic of China.[4] Since then, a Chinese judge too has been ensconced at the ICJ permanently. There has never been a case of a permanent member losing an ICJ election.

Also, if the convention of the distribution of seats among various regions is followed, then too the UK is favoured. There is no instance of a seat held by a judge from a particular region being won by a judge from another region.

However, this is not any non-member of the Council that has a candidate in the fray. As Lord Ahmad later graciously acknowledges in his testimony to the UK Parliament's Foreign Affairs Committee, 'In the final run-off, it was very much about how people perceived India.'[5] This is our belief too. If the prevalent perception of India's status as an emerging power is a factor, it will be hard for the UK to overcome an Indian candidate in the General Assembly. The results, as they are announced simultaneously in both the Security Council and the General Assembly, are a fair reflection of the relative strengths of the two countries in each of the bodies.[6]

Candidate	COUNTRY		
		SC	GA
Dalveer Bhandari	INDIA	6	115
Christopher Greenwood	UK	9	76
TOTAL VOTES CAST TOTAL VOTES AVAILABLE		15 15	191 192

Judge Greenwood scores better in the Security Council, as was to be expected. The five permanent members have a cosy, long-standing unwritten arrangement that they will always vote for each other irrespective of the credentials of any opponent. It was the modern-day version of the Latin phrase 'Unus pro omnibus, omnes pro uno'. A French version, 'Un pour tous, tous pour un', that means 'One for all, all for one', was made famous by Alexandre Dumas in his 1844 novel *Les Trois Mousquetaires— The Three Musketeers*.

Any candidate from a permanent member country always begins with five votes in the kitty, so only ten elected members' votes are available to the opponent. That Judge Bhandari secures six of the ten is creditable. The fact that Judge Greenwood gets his support from four of the ten elected members is indicative of where the sympathies of those elected through the General Assembly lie. It is enough to indicate that Judge Bhandari has strong support when the playing field is even, but not enough to surmount the carefully crafted advantage that the permanent members have on their turf—the Security Council.

In the General Assembly, the thirty-nine-vote lead that Judge Bhandari chalks up is huge. Judge Greenwood has fallen below the required majority of ninety-seven votes by twenty-one from the 191 valid votes that are cast. Every historical precedent suggests that such a difference in the General Assembly can never be surmounted. On the other hand, many have overcome larger deficits than Judge Bhandari's in the Security Council to win. More importantly, we have studied our history of ICJ elections well. The conventional wisdom is that in case of a divergence in the outcomes of direct elections in the General Assembly and the Security Council for a seat on the ICJ, the General Assembly inevitably prevails.[7]

There is only one limited derogation of sorts in this scheme in the past. In 2008, Judge Abdulqawi Ahmed Yusuf (Somalia) was contesting for the last seat of the five on offer against Miriam Defensor Santiago (Philippines) and Maurice Kamto (Cameroon). He had polled less than the Filipino judge in the General Assembly in the first ballot. If the trend had continued, an Asian judge would have succeeded an African judge. That had never happened ever before. In the subsequent ballots, the 'deviation' was corrected. Judge Yusuf gained the lead in the General Assembly from the second ballot onwards. He finally won and Africa retained the seat that was previously held by Judge Raymond Ranjeva (Madagascar).[8] The convention has always prevailed.

Sitting in the General Assembly at the India desk, I find myself wondering whether the natural disposition of forces has put us on the cusp of making history, or will our effort be derailed like that of the Filipino judge in 2008? I soon realize that such thinking betrays naïveté. There is still a long path ahead that we need to traverse. The first indication of this comes soon.

Both the presidents of the General Assembly and the Security Council conclude their respective meetings for the day although the afternoon session started an hour later than usual. Also, both announce simultaneously that the next vote will be held after four days, on the afternoon of 13 November 2017. This is contrary to the dates (9 and 10 November) that have been announced as being set aside for ICJ elections. This departure is immediately noticed by several supportive ambassadors who rush to me and point out that it may have been designed to provide space for the UK and its supporters to garner support by approaching capitals. 'Challenge this change. It is contrary to what has been announced and is without any consultation. We will support you,' they urge.

It is entirely correct that 9 and 10 November had been set aside many days ago for the conduct of the ICJ elections. The change in the dates and the setting of a new date has not even been mentioned to us before this announcement. It is also true that the UK has, over the years, established strong linkages with the UN Secretariat. The possibility that the change is in consultation with them cannot be discounted. On the other hand, I feel that we should not be distracted by such procedural manoeuvres. 'This is not our forte. If we venture there, it will be tantamount to playing on an unfamiliar playing field,' I respond to those who are calling for a protest. 'Let it pass,' I tell them. I can see that they are visibly disappointed with my response. 'Engaging in such skirmishes will dissipate our energies,' I explain. It will shift our focus from what matters most—that is, capitalizing on the unparalleled opportunity that we have been presented with. Unseating a permanent member in an election to the principal judicial organ of the United Nations has never happened before. We need to focus on that goal to the exclusion of all else.

If the UK and its supporters feel that the few days that the delay provides will bring into play their broader outreach in capitals across the globe, it means that they are tacitly acknowledging that efforts in New York will not be able to change the disposition of delegates significantly. They and others are underestimating India's global outreach work undertaken over the past few months. In fact, it is the efforts of Indian missions and diplomats engaging with interlocutors globally that has kept us in the game so far, despite our announcing our candidature much later than all the other countries. If they want us to up our game further, it is their choice. We are ready to do so. If they want us to do so everywhere, so be it. We were prepared for a fight to the finish.

———∞∞∞———

There are matters that need to be addressed immediately. The voting for seats on the ICJ is by secret ballot. However, in multilateral diplomacy, there are very few secrets. More so in the case of the Security Council. Like a cosy club, the fifteen members have a fairly good idea where each stands on an issue. The more engaged Permanent Representatives from amongst Council members are usually able to fathom even the secrets of voting in the Council based on their conversations and a bit of scouting by their delegates. I set out to seek the insights of a few of them.

'Something fishy was going on,' says a Security Council diplomat summing up the day's proceedings. Having sat through all the votes in the Council, he had a ringside view of the goings on. 'India is a large and respected country with many friends. However, you were done in by your friends pursuing loftier goals,' he says, pointing to a shift in two Council votes after the lunch recess. 'The total votes remained as they were in the round previous to that ... but two votes were shifted from you to another candidate from your region by a regional group to help a candidate from their region,' is his assessment. 'It was not that they liked India less; it was simply a case that they liked their region more,' is his pithy conclusion, alluding to Brutus's justification for turning against Julius Caesar. It makes sense. It seems to fit in with the facts and it is in tune with our own concerns about group loyalties. Yet, it is only one sophisticated diplomat's hypothesis with no corroboration. The answer to which two countries in the Security Council shifted their votes away from India perhaps lies at my next port of call.

Since most UN missions are located very close to each other, and such is my eagerness to better understand the Council dynamics, I visit another colleague less than ten minutes after he agrees to meet me at the end of a long day of voting. In his assessment, 'The distillation process is over. The choice now is between a developing country that is clearly on the rise and a developed country which had contributed much but is past its best. Complicating issues of individual friendships, regional interests and prior commitments, which weighed in the earlier multi-cornered votes, are no longer in the mix. You can count on us now.'

When, half in jest, I query that he seems to emphasize on the now, he parries with, 'You need to appreciate the dynamics of evolving situations. Now, even your good friends—old and new—Russia and Japan are not with you.' Then he lowers his voice and with a mischievous grin adds, 'I know this as, unlike in the General Assembly, Council delegates are seated much closer. It helps us understand each other better.' He then concludes with, 'Let me assure you: irrespective of the past, we will be with you all the way now.'

It is the closest I can come to getting a confirmation that he is part of the group that switched votes to sink us, ensuring that a candidate from their region swam through. I thank him, even though a part of me is yelling loudly inside: 'Et tu, Brute?' His advice that we must let bygones be bygones is sound. His information of old and new friends pursuing their own interests is brutal but frank. His willingness to now be with us is reassuring. It is time to put this to rest. Together, we have bigger fish to fry now. Diplomacy demands, as does life itself, that rather than looking back and nursing wounds of the past, it is best to keep looking ahead in pursuit of cherished goals.

Indian judges of the International Court of Justice: (from top) Dr B.N. Rau (right), 1952-53, died in office; Dr Nagendra Singh, 1973–88, died in office; R.S. Pathak (centre), 1989–91, elected to the seat that became vacant on account of Dr Singh's death for the remainder of the term.

Incumbent judges of the ICJ had never faced each other in a direct electoral contest until Judge Christopher Greenwood of the UK (seated, extreme right) and Judge Dalveer Bhandari of India (standing, third from right) did in 2017.

Judge Dalveer Bhandari

INDIA'S CANDIDATE FOR THE INTERNATIONAL COURT OF JUSTICE

ICJ Judge since April 2012

Previous Experience

Judge at the Supreme Court of India
Chief Justice of High Court of Mumbai
Judge at High Court of Delhi
Attorney at Law for over two decades
Professor Emeritus of Law

A pamphlet promoting Judge Bhandari's candidature.

Election campaigns at the UN are a blur of meet-and-greet events that require judges to press the flesh just as other candidates do. (From top) Judge Bhandari with the Permanent Representative of Israel (it was the first time that Israel nominated a non-national candidate to the ICJ); with the Permanent Representative of Uzbekistan, India's first pledged voter; and with the Permanent Representative of Colombia.

(From top) Judge Bhandari with the Permanent Representative of Japan; with the Permanent Representative of Oman; the final meet-and-greet as India and the UK entered the last round of voting.

This meeting between Prime Minister Narendra Modi and President Shavkat Mirziyoyev of Uzbekistan on 9 June 2017 in Astana (now known as Nur Sultan), Kazakhstan, on the fringes of the Shanghai Cooperation Organization Summit, led to the first pledge of support for Judge Bhandari's ICJ candidature.

External Affairs Minister Sushma Swaraj indefatigably canvassed for support for the Indian candidate to the ICJ during the UN's annual General Assembly session in September 2017.

The elections to the ICJ are unique, with the UN General Assembly and the Security Council voting simultaneously for the same candidates.

As the final denouement approached, the missions of the UK and India engaged in a ferocious tussle while their leaders made frenetic phone calls drumming up support for their candidates.

The moment following the formal announcement of success.

Election officer Anjani Kumar takes a selfie to capture the essence of a victorious moment.

Judge Bhandari, Mrs Madhu Bhandari, Ambassador Tanmaya Lal and I join Indian mission staff in celebrating the unprecedented victory.

The trench warriors savour the ICJ victory in their 'karma bhoomi', the UN's General Assembly Hall.

8

I Punished Them the Only Way I Could

SEEMINGLY SIMPLE INNOVATIONS sometimes tend to be more handy than established mechanisms. The seamless digital communications platform, set up at the initiative of Director Vinod Jacob a few months ago, is now buzzing constantly as all senior Indian diplomats are catching up to its utility. Foreign Secretary Dr Jaishankar, as usual, is the first off the blocks and is seeking more precise inputs about the overall situation. Vijay Gokhale, who had until recently been our Ambassador in Beijing and has taken over as Secretary (Economic Relations) in the latter half of October, is, as always, quick on the ball. He is already responding to our recommendations for further outreach with a few Arab and African states and is providing feedback based on his interactions. Secretary (West) Ruchi Ghanashyam is asking for information about the European states that need to be shored up in the changed circumstances, where one of their own is in a direct contest with us. Secretary (East) Preeti Saran is departing for Manila to join the annual ASEAN Summit meetings and wants to know which delegations she needs to pursue there. Over the course of the next ten days, the common digital platform becomes the go-to tool for rapid communications, even as more conventional systems continue to be used for sensitive inputs.

External Affairs Minister Sushma Swaraj has a series of telephone conversations with me all through the day. She is posing searching questions and seeking detailed responses on what our chances of success are in the new race. 'It is one thing for you to take a spur-of-the-moment decision and engage in an unanticipated contest by chance. However, I now need to make a careful choice, taking into account every aspect,' she says. As is her usual style, she indicates that she is also consulting others with experience and understanding of UN matters. 'The signals are mixed [...] I have checked with many of your predecessors. Their feeling is that at the UN, you can't take on a permanent member and win such a contest. It is tantamount to tilting at windmills according to some,' she ominously adds. Then, she helpfully mentions, 'However, all of the senior officials of the Ministry of External Affairs are in unison supporting the recommendation to proceed.' Finally, she concludes in a lighter vein, 'Don't worry, I will be Don Quixote and lead the charge. You can be Sancho Panza.' I take it that this is her way of signalling that we can proceed full throttle and assuring me that she is taking full responsibility.

Once the political direction is provided, the diplomatic establishment sets the global wheels of Indian diplomacy in motion again. The heads of the territorial divisions at the headquarters are directing Indian missions globally to swiftly reach out at the highest possible level to seek support. Resident missions in Delhi too are being pursued diligently. We, at the permanent mission, are naturally doing our bit. As we gather for a detailed debriefing session in the morning, the young and talented bunch of diplomats at the mission are all buoyant and full of ideas. Not for nothing has the Indian mission to the UN been known for decades as the nursery of Indian diplomacy. It attracts bright and exceptionally diligent young diplomats who are required to pursue, on a daily basis, India's national interests and marry them to globally acceptable outcomes. In the process, they learn to respond independently to evolving situations and gain confidence to take decisions in difficult circumstances after assessing different perspectives. Now is their test to prove their worth.

First Secretary Mahesh Kumar, who had anticipated 'tactical voting' by some members of the Arab group, suggests, 'Please try and re-engage with key Arab ambassadors, including Palestine's long-time observer, Ambassador Riyad Mansoor, and the newly elected Lebanese ICJ judge, Nawaf Salam, so as to allay their concerns about Judge Bhandari being Israel's candidate.'

First Secretary Ashish Sinha warns, 'The UK has initiated a whisper campaign that, given the strength of bilateral ties, India will not stand in the way of the UK taking its permanent perch on the ICJ.' He then adds, 'We should nip such talk in the bud or it will draw support away from us.'

First Secretary Sandeep Kumar, who had served in Beijing and is now our point person on Security Council issues, advises, 'We should consistently engage at all levels with each of the permanent members, even though this will not wean any of them away from supporting the UK. However, it may help in their not deciding to coordinate every move together and collectively work against us in a vigorous manner.'

Counsellor Anjani Kumar is worried about our limited logistical resources. He proposes, 'Let us seek reinforcements to improve our "ground game".' He even has the names of two of his predecessor election officers at the mission—Counsellor Devesh Uttam from Tehran and Counsellor Manjunath from Colombo—as candidates to be requisitioned since they know many delegates.

First Secretary Eenam Gambhir feels, 'We need to expand our media outreach in India as the election is at an inflection point, and we need to sensitize public opinion in India about the situation.'

Legal Adviser Umasankar volunteers to look at legal pathways that the UK may venture upon to come out of the 'political blackhole' in which they are. He then sets about explaining that Greenwood had in October 2002 tendered a controversial legal opinion to the British government on the 'Legality of Using Force Against Iraq',[1] when he was an academic. He is understood to have argued that the original resolutions passed against Saddam Hussein after the Kuwait war of 1990 provided a basis for action if the Security Council so determined, as would a determination by the UK of an imminent threat from an Iraq with weapons of mass destruction capabilities. This is an assessment that critics consider a minority legal view. It also seems to have contradicted much of the advice that the UK foreign office was providing to the country's attorney general. Several UK members of parliament had consequently objected to his nomination in 2008 as the nation's candidate to the ICJ. 'While these are issues of the past, they highlight the individual's legal philosophy and approach to global issues,' sums up our legal eagle.

Counsellor Mayank Joshi, who had served the longest amongst us in New York, argues, 'The competition is now along several of the established fault lines in the UN system—the General Assembly's role vis-à-vis that of the Security Council, the notion of developed country versus developing country, the concerns about the "cascade" effect, which are viewed as a form of expansion of the permanence of the permanent members into areas which are not specified in the UN Charter.' According to him, 'In all these divides, our position is in tune with the broad majority.' Even in the case of regional group support, the UK can only expect majority support from the West and East European groups, which together constitute about fifty members. Hence, 'in every contest of numbers we stand to gain, if we play to our strengths' is his conclusion.

First Secretary Paulomi Tripathi, who had been added to the team a few months ago, draws upon her administrative experience at the headquarters and suggests, 'We should follow the dictum of the Roman emperor Marcus Aurelius that every task we are required to fulfil has to be approached as the most important thing each of us is required to do.' We need to ensure perfection in fulfilling our designated work, she concludes.

Our military adviser, Colonel Sandeep Kapoor, chips in with a sporting analogy. He narrates the practice of the legendary US National Football League coach Bill Belichick, who always emphasizes to his players: 'Do your job.' The UN has hundreds of issues at any given time. 'So, each of us should keep our focus only on the task allocated, otherwise we can get lost in other people's business,' he says.

With so much sagacious advice and so many action points put on the table, the task for seniors like Tanmaya and me is rather easy. We need to pursue as many of the numerous good suggestions as possible that this group of thoughtful diplomats has provided us with.

Saturday, 11 November 2017
New York

'What are your plans?' asks the UK's Permanent Representative Matthew Rycroft on the telephone. While we have a cordial relationship, this is the first time I am hearing from him over a weekend. 'We hope to win' is my response. 'But, not in the Council' is his swift repartee. The feeling I get is that the UK is nervous but unwilling to contemplate that they can lose. Rather than get into an argument, I suggest that we keep this 'private line' that he has initiated going. We then talk about the vagaries of the election process that has led to our two candidates being the only ones left. We end by agreeing to keep in touch. In a hotly contested election, things become difficult and it is always good diplomatic practice to keep a channel open in case we see scope for a mutually acceptable outcome.

In the meanwhile, despite the limited time available, Minister Swaraj is making calls to key counterparts. Many of our ambassadors are pitching in at every level possible. Our senior officers in Delhi are continuously working with resident ambassadors. When required, we even seek the help of Joint Secretary Gopal Baglay in the Prime Minister's Office to get Prime Minister Modi to put in a word. The responses that pour in from our missions are overwhelmingly encouraging.

As we venture on the diplomatic version of a 'full court press', we come across several complications that unanticipated contests of the nature that we are involved in can pose for others. In one case, a National Group had responded to our request and at a meeting confirmed support for Judge Bhandari before the election. The Permanent Representative of the country who had suggested this pathway for us to seek approval of his National Group is now in a dilemma. Judge Greenwood is a friend and classmate of his. However, their National Group has not endorsed him, since it was taken for granted that he did not require such support. Being a nominee of a P-5 state, it was assumed that he would win easily. Hence, neither had he approached the National Group for such endorsement nor had it discussed the matter. National commitment now clashed with personal friendship.

In another case, a Permanent Representative from a developing country had made a written reciprocal arrangement to support Judge Bhandari in every round, in return for our commitment to do similarly for the ambassador's own candidature next year in a very important election. Now the ambassador's personal interest is clashing with their government's support for Judge Greenwood; since he had been their counsel in the past, they couldn't desert him in his hour of need.

Some responses, both in the capitals and in New York, take us by surprise. Uruguay, which had voted in the Security Council for us, is now thinking that it is not in its best interests to continue to do so. Their mission in New York has suggested that they abstain during future votes. Since we do not have a diplomatic presence in Montevideo, it will be only next week that our ambassador in Buenos Aires can meet his Uruguayan counterparts to see if they can review this. It is a setback, but not fatal.

We have not charted our pathway to victory directly through a change in the votes in the Security Council. Our plan is different. We want to increase our votes in the General Assembly in such a manner that it will be difficult for the UK to sustain its candidature in view of the mounting difference in the votes between the two candidates. Our target is to get two-thirds of the general membership to vote for us. Once we get to this objective, we feel that some in the Council will switch sides, especially since there are eight Council members who are consistently telling us that they are voting for us but two of the eight are in fact voting for the other candidate. Our focus, therefore, principally is on the votes in the General Assembly. The presumption is that the Security Council numbers will follow.

In the Council, we probe Japan; our bilateral relations are excellent, as is our engagement at the UN, since we both are part of the G-4 that consists of Brazil, Germany, India and Japan and aims to work collectively on the reform of the Security Council. Alas, even ten years after Prime Minister Shinzo Abe's announcement in the Indian Parliament that the 'Japan–India relationship is blessed with the largest potential for development of any bilateral relationship anywhere in the world',[2] Japan never shows a semblance of willingness to even consider supporting us. They just freeze us out, declining every overture to discuss the issue—at any stage—once India and the UK stumble into a contest. On the other hand, Brazil, another G-4 partner, is a stalwart ally and Ambassador Mauro Vieira is amongst the most vocal in support for us and in seeking the support of others on our behalf.

Ambassador Nawaf Salam, fresh from his success, explains that he is abstaining in the direct contest as whoever wins will join him as a judge at the ICJ. I acknowledge the optics from his personal standpoint although we were seeking Lebanon's support, not his vote as an individual. Nevertheless, it is better to have an abstention than a negative vote.

Israel, which had nominated Judge Bhandari as a non-national candidate before, is now taking an inordinate amount of time to respond. It is making us wonder whether we have lost Israel. We have already lost some others on account of Israel's prior announced support.

Sunday, 12 November 2017
New York

If some important partners in the developed world have their own priorities, such is our range of partners that numerous others can be counted upon to support us. It is developing countries the world over that are the most responsive. Most Pacific states reconfirm support promptly, with Ambassador Vishvas Sapkal happily reporting that he has reconfirmations from six UN members he is accredited to. The enthusiasm of many Caribbean states too is heart-warming, though many prefer not to make their support vocal on account of the strong Commonwealth links to the UK. Similarly, even some Arab states with strong ties to the UK discretely convey support in New Delhi to Dr Bala Bhaskar, who is coordinating our outreach to the Arab world. Most African states remain steadfast, as do our friendly neighbours.

More good news follows. Israel's Ambassador Danny Danon confirms continued support after seeking and receiving instructions at the 'highest level'. Palestine, which does not have a vote but whose voice carries weight in some quarters, had in the past viewed Israeli support for Judge Bhandari with concern. They now respond to our outreach and inform us that, following consultation with their authorities, they have received instructions to weigh in with their friends to support India.

For the UK, Secretary of State Boris Johnson is on the phone shoring up support and seeking new commitments during contacts with his counterparts, according to several Latin American and Caribbean ambassadors. In New York, the UK is not averse to leveraging Council membership with some members who had issues on the Council's agenda. An ambassador who narrates this to me mentions that it was 'traumatic' when a UK diplomat, in an encounter in the Council chambers, reminded her of their need for the UK if their issue comes up. 'It is the UK—and not India—which will matter then, as India is not even on the Council.' Nevertheless, the warning is ignored and they decide to stay the course and continue to support us.

Another Permanent Representative candidly accepts that they are obliged to change their stance in favour of the UK. 'Our situation is such that the UK's help on the Council is important for us.' Such tactics by Security Council members are par for the course. Our own stance in support of Mauritius on the issue of the Chagos archipelago, as the only non-African country to speak in support of the African Union resolution in the summer of 2017, is referred to by many African states as a factor in reiterating their steadfast support.

Judge Bhandari, who has been present on the sidelines observing the proceedings with stoic detachment thus far despite the swings in his fortunes, is effusive. 'I have never seen such sustained dedication,' he says about the efforts being put in by all of us on his behalf. During our conversation, I provide him examples of some of the responses linked with Judge Greenwood's personal contacts. Judge Bhandari listens intently and expresses willingness—even eagerness—to be actively engaged. I respond, 'It is part of our job,' and mention that although 'we as diplomats will get muddied', he should remain above the fray as he has scrupulously done till now. I explain that it is in his best interests as it enhances his persona as the archetypal independent judge not personally beholden to anyone, even in trying circumstances.

Our assessment on the eve of the voting day is that despite all their efforts, the UK is nowhere near overturning the lead we have. We hope to hold the lead in the General Assembly and even increase it. In the Security Council, no change is envisaged, except for Uruguay's abstention.

So far, not many beyond diplomats and foreign office officials have taken note of the battle that India is engaging on the multilateral stage. Persisting with her belief that we need broader outreach, First Secretary Eenam Gambhir of her own accord sets up a telephone conversation for me with Dr Shashi Tharoor, the former Minister of State for External Affairs and consummate UN insider who had served as Under Secretary General. He is now an opposition Member of Parliament chairing the Parliamentary Committee on External Affairs. Although it is late in the evening, she contacts Dr Tharoor's office and insists that I call him right then and seek his help to increase public outreach.

Dr Tharoor is travelling in Central Asia. He readily takes the call at the airport just before emplaning for another destination in Europe. He is sceptical if his speaking out will help. Nonetheless, he agrees to sensitize public opinion on the matter. What follows is a 'tweet storm'. @ShashiTharoor launches a series of seven tweets explaining the contours of the developments at the UN and plugging in with a call to 'vote4India'.[3] While most Twitterati are not voters, Dr Tharoor's large social media following ensures that the Indian media starts taking considerably more interest in the issue.

⁂

Monday, 13 November 2017
New York

The UK has realized the gravity of the situation. Lord Ahmad of Wimbledon, the Minister of State for Commonwealth and the United Nations,[4] is rushed to New York, diverting him from a visit to the Caribbean. The entire morning of the election day, he is frenetically lobbying delegates all over the UN. The affable life peer of South Asian descent that he is, in his meeting with me Lord Ahmad is at pains to emphasize the cordiality of ties with India.

First Secretary Ashish Sinha immediately sees this as reinforcing his own fears of the UK's game plan. Later that afternoon, whenever Lord Ahmad approaches me in the General Assembly Hall in between the votes, young Ashish comes over, draws me aside and even admonishes me for not heeding his advice. For the rest of that afternoon, contrary to my usual style, he ensures that I am at the far side of the General Assembly, away from Ambassador Rycroft and Lord Ahmad. India's young diplomats have taken ownership of the election process.

Going into the vote, there is a discordant note. We have confirmation that US diplomats and lawyers are actively canvassing for the UK among a selected list of Asian, African and Latin American states. Since the weekend of 11–12 November has intervened, our legal adviser, Umasankar, only gets whiff of it a little before the vote. The US mission to the

UN has mailed about forty missions asking them to vote for the UK and terming a vote for India as disruptive of the established arrangements. The communication argues that India's win will be against the interest of every regional group and detrimental to every country's aspirations in the long run, besides a loss for the ICJ itself in terms of legal traditions. The US is batting solidly not only for the UK but also for the continuance of the existing order. It sees India as a threat to the stability of the established dispensation at the United Nations. A threat it does not want to see succeed.

A former senior US diplomat, who had served in New Delhi during the first decade of the twenty-first century and had played a visible role during the India–US nuclear deal negotiations, is also fielded to gain support for the UK amongst our neighbours. The diplomat, who portrays himself as a 'friend' of India, and occasionally writes in leading Indian newspapers about the imperatives of India–US friendship, is known to many Indian diplomats. Upon my joining as Permanent Representative, he was introduced to me by a senior Indian diplomat who was then stationed at our embassy in Washington, DC. The retired US diplomat is usually requisitioned as an adviser to the US mission to the UN during the September–December period. This 'friend' is approaching several of our neighbours and urging them to vote against us and in favour of the UK. With 'friends' like him actively working overtime against us, who needs enemies?

It is not a matter of hearsay alone. Ambassador Rohan Pereira, a veteran public international lawyer who is the Sri Lankan Permanent Representative, recalls that the Sri Lankan stance is that Asia requires one more seat on the ICJ. This dates back to the 1990s, when Sri Lanka's Judge Weeramantry[5] (who had succeeded Judge Pathak of India in 1991) was in the fray. He recounts that his response to the US South Asia specialist is that 'what Sri Lanka began more than two decades ago is now on the verge of being realized, thanks to India'.

Several other South Asian ambassadors too recount conversations with this so-called friend when I seek confirmation. They also reassure me that they are not swayed at all. They are our true friends indeed.

We have confirmation from multiple interlocutors. It is too late to do anything before the vote. Tanmaya and I confer and decide that the legal adviser should not share any of this with any of our young colleagues, lest it demoralizes them in any way.

The voting is a crucial test of whether Indian diplomacy can withstand the onslaught. We are confronting the UK's global efforts. It has raised the pitch in New York with high-level political oversight, in an arena where it is ensconced as a key player for seventy years. The explicit overtures, made by the US mission in New York to a list of those who had voted for India but could be persuaded to change their votes, mean they feel that the US and the UK working together can turn the tide. In addition, we are battling two historical precedents. Permanent members usually have a permanent presence on the ICJ, and the informal regional balance of seats that reflects the geographical distribution of seats on the ICJ, as in the case of the Security Council, has remained undisturbed for decades. On the other hand, we have approached this with quiet confidence. While all of our diplomats are working globally, and our top leadership is fully engaged, we are essentially on our own—facing a mighty combination of global powers who also have history on their side.

Coming into the General Assembly Hall, the sight of Second Secretary Mohammed Afsar and his logistical team spreading out to all corners of the cavernous hall, distributing the brochure seeking support for Judge Bhandari, makes me forget, albeit temporarily, the blow that the US mission has dealt us. Our young diplomats seem all over the place, meeting their designated interlocutors and putting in a final word.

That such overtures matter is affirmed by a seasoned Latin American ambassador. He is from a country where we have no resident mission and no contact established through the capitals; but attention was lavished on him by us in New York. Despite Ashish Sinha piloting me to distant corners during the interregnums between the votes, the exuberant Latin diplomat buttonholes me after the end of the fourth round and animatedly explains that earlier during the day, his foreign minister had called him and asked him to vote for the UK. Accordingly, he had voted for the UK for three rounds. However, no UK diplomat even requested him for his vote, while several of ours approached him after every round. He had also noticed that many times senior UK officials had come across and talked to me during the brief intervals when votes were being counted, while neglecting him.

Hence, 'I punished them the only way I could,' he concludes. Then, as an afterthought, he smiles and adds, 'And you, my friend, are the beneficiary.' Votes tend to change between one round and another—sometimes for substantive reasons, at other times for purely stylistic ones.

Since only two candidates are in the fray, the voting process takes a much shorter time than on the first day. In the course of less than three hours, there are five rounds of votes, independently but simultaneously in the Security

Council and the General Assembly. The cumulative impact of the UK's efforts globally and in New York, and the US and the UK working in concert in New York, is that at the end of the day they are worse off than at the beginning. Our global outreach has paid dividends. Second Secretary Lakshmi Swaminathan, who is monitoring the voting and plotting the results against past votes in such circumstances, shows me a quick comparative table of the situation in the election between Argentina and Jamaica in 2014. She says that the voting is 'eerily similar in both cases' and projects that if voting continues for two more rounds, we will be achieving our objective. It is not to be so. Objective data may be similar, but diplomatic responses need not be so.

At the end of five rounds, we are where Jamaica was at the end of four rounds in the General Assembly in 2014. We have one vote less in the Security Council than when we began. The UK is where Argentina was at the same juncture in both the General Assembly and the Security Council. Yet, the voting could not continue for two more rounds as it did in 2014. The 'dramatis personae' now are different. The voting ends at round five with the announcement that it will be resumed 'at a date to be announced later'. The ostensible reason is a social event that one of the presiding officers is to host outside the UN.

Nevertheless, the trajectory of where the election is heading, whenever the process is resumed, is not lost on us. The balloting has proved that there is no deviation in the general membership's support for India. We have out-polled the UK in five direct contests in the General Assembly—in fact six, if the single direct contest on 9 November is added. We are fifty-three votes ahead of the UK in the General Assembly, and three votes short of an absolute majority in the

Candidate	COUNTRY	Round 1		Round 2		Round 3		Round 4		Round 5		Round 6		Round 7	
		SC	GA	SC	GA	SC	GA	SC	GA	SC	GA	SC	GA	SC	GA
	2017														
Dalveer Bhandari	INDIA	5	110	5	113	5	111	5	118		121				
Christopher Greenwood	UK	9	79	9	76	9	79	9	72		68				
	2014														
Susana Ruiz Cerutti	Argentina	9	77	9	71	9	69	9	68	9	65	9	64	9	61
Patrick Lipton Robinson	Jamaica	6	115	6	121	6	123	6	121	6	125	6	127	6	130

Security Council. Conversely, the UK is in danger of falling below the absolute majority required in the Council by just two votes. Exactly the position where we were in terms of numbers during the lunch break on the first day of voting on 9 November, a ballot before we fell below the absolute majority. If the election continues, previous trends point that there is only one possible outcome.

As we are to depart from the General Assembly Hall at the end of the day, I look to the visitors' gallery to brief Judge Bhandari, as usual, before leaving. When I look towards the gallery, where the only two judges who remain in the fray are seated, I see that one of them is in conversation with Pakistani Permanent Representative Ambassador Maleeha Lodhi. It is Judge Greenwood. Rather than interrupt the conversation that Judge Greenwood is having while Judge Bhandari is sitting pensively nearby, I wait at our desk. Very few delegates are left in the hall. Looking around, I see that several Pakistani delegates are still present around their desk and are talking amongst themselves. Since it is not the first time that so many delegates from Pakistan are still in the hall well after the ICJ voting, I am wondering why.

My senior colleague Srinivas, who usually keeps to himself, seems to read my thoughts. He comes over and explains that Judge Greenwood has an impressive portfolio as an international arbitrator even while serving on the ICJ. He explains that there are growing concerns of ICJ judges functioning as international arbitrators especially in cases of investor-state disputes. While it may seem strange, there is no prohibition that restricts them from doing so.[6] Hesitating a little, he goes on to add that there is speculation that Judge Greenwood earns more through his international arbitration role than in his ICJ role, and there is criticism that he is moonlighting.[7]

Then he mentions, 'Pakistan's interest in the contest is not only limited to not wanting to have India on the ICJ. Judge Greenwood has rendered legal services to Pakistan before he joined the ICJ.' He was the Pakistani counsel in two commercial arbitration cases.[8] I leave thinking to myself that if victory comes, it will be doubly delightful.

9

Let Us Leave It

———⊷∞∞⊶———

Wednesday, 15 November 2017
New York

A S IS OFTEN said, where you stand will determine what you see. Then again, who you stand with will determine what you hear. And what you see and hear will determine what you say and how you act.

The same facts are being viewed in entirely different ways by those in different situations. We perceive the outcome of the second day of voting as a clear step forward on the pathway we have chalked towards victory. The UK and some others among us seem to think it is a vindication of the view that the vote, with different outcomes in the Security Council and the General Assembly, reinforces the initial stalemate at the end of the first day.

The 'private line' that Ambassador Matthew Rycroft and I have is not going anywhere. The conversations we have are mere reiteration of our respective perceptions. He keeps pointing to our inability to make progress in the Security Council and suggests that we consider withdrawing. I insist that the repeated rounds of defeat in the General Assembly are denting Judge Greenwood's credibility and the next few rounds will establish conclusively the burgeoning support for

Judge Bhandari amongst the general membership of the UN. Even as we talk, both of us are planning our separate ways forward.

For our part, we continue our global outreach in readiness for the next round. The Minister of External Affairs is pursuing her telephone exchanges with gusto. Every time there is an input that Foreign Secretary Boris Johnson of the UK has called up a counterpart, Swaraj's office tries to engage that specific counterpart too, in addition to the many others she has on her list. In a week, she has made more than forty telephone calls[1] to every corner of the globe, sometimes catching her counterparts while they are travelling elsewhere.

The UN divisions of the Ministry of External Affairs in New Delhi are working overtime, providing all our missions with updated results and 'talking points' emphasizing that we count on the continued backing of our supporters at the next round. The other two ministers of state, General V.K. Singh and M.J. Akbar, are also roped in wherever necessary. The senior officials of the ministry—Dr Jaishankar, Vijay Gokhale, Ruchi Ghanashyam and Preeti Saran—remain engaged with resident ambassadors in Delhi and are directing some of our key ambassadors to reach out at the highest possible levels. Rarely, perhaps, has the focus of Indian diplomats globally been on one multilateral election in such a manner ever before. All of the requirements for additional personnel and financial resources needed by us in New York are promptly agreed to. Such intensity of engagement and responsiveness is unprecedented.

However, a senior colleague, who is participating in the strategy sessions that Minister Swaraj is personally presiding over every day in New Delhi, warns me, 'All of us are pushing this to the maximum. It can't last for long. You better work on a breakthrough. Your window of opportunity is closing.' He is reflecting what many others, even in our mission, are already thinking out loud too.

Every day, we have two internal meetings at the mission in New York to understand better the responses that each of us is receiving from other delegations. While the general feeling is that we have gained the upper hand, the divide is about whether this is enough to ensure a victory. Several of those who usually handle political issues, including Security Council matters, are arguing that we need to be 'realistic' and 'pragmatic'. 'We have already achieved much more than what any member of the UN had done. We have out-polled a permanent member by considerable margins six times amongst the general membership. Even amongst the elected members of the Security Council, the UK has never out-polled us once,' they argue. They suggest we proclaim a 'moral victory' and 'cut a deal'. It is said that the influence of the P-5 on the thinking of all UN diplomats is pervasive. This is reflecting in the thinking of some of our very best too.

With every passing day, votaries of such 'realistic' thinking are gaining ground all around. According to them, there is 'no other way' forward. I hear this repeatedly and increasingly in my conversations with colleagues from Delhi. On the other hand, the counter-argument in the mission is perhaps best articulated by First Secretary Ashish Sinha. 'Of what real use is a moral victory?' is his stout defence of the need to persevere. 'It is unrealistic for us to package our inability to get a judge re-elected as a moral victory and then expect to sell this as an acceptable outcome,' is First Secretary Paulomi Tripathi's opposition to any deal-making that does not entail re-election of Judge Bhandari. Significantly, both have limited exposure to the functioning of the Security Council. Perhaps for that reason, they are bolder in their willingness to keep going, even against a P-5 member. On the other hand, Minister Swaraj, who is in touch with Indian diplomats with years of previous UN experience, says that the 'old-timers' whom she has consulted are also in different ways hinting that it is 'time to cut a deal'.

Ordinarily such back-and-forth debates are indicative of the intellectual vibrancy of decision-making. However, the need for 'closure' to the issue is permeating across many colleagues in Delhi and also all our staff. My personal secretary, Vaidyanathan, who invariably works late hours and is the last to leave the office after seeing me off late at night, once joins in support saying, 'Sir, we all have worked so hard for so long; maybe we should now share the seat and end this business.' I realize that the desire for a satisfying outcome is corroding our belief that we can win. Patience is reaching its limits everywhere. We need some indications that the tide is turning in our favour if we are to stem the creeping desire for instant outcomes.

At times, shifts—however small—come when least expected and from unlikely quarters. Mauritius's Permanent Representative, Ambassador Jagdish Kunjal, is extremely well versed with ICJ issues and keeps in touch with various public international lawyers handling a variety of cases. He is a repository of knowledge about the inclination of various countries and the ties of individuals, including Judge Greenwood, with various governments, lawyers and arbitrators, as also those who differ from him. Mauritius had objected to Judge Greenwood's appointment as an arbitrator in a case at the Permanent Court of Arbitration relating to the Chagos archipelago under Annex VII of the United Nations Convention on the Law of the Seas.[2] I seek his counsel. Drawing upon the wealth of his experience, the soft-spoken, long-time diplomat provides invaluable pointers on arbitration issues relating to Judge Greenwood and about the path to traverse in reaching out to the top-level leaders in various countries, including Uruguay, to restore their vote in support of Judge Bhandari. Pursuing this path, we are able to make some progress. Uruguay, we are told, is veering towards reverting to its initial position in the next round. Uruguay, a Latin American member of the Security Council, had moved from an initial vote in our support to an abstention. Now, it is likely to move from an abstention to an affirmative vote for us in the Security Council. It is a small step. Nevertheless, it is significant. It signals that states are rethinking their votes in the Council in light of the strong showing by us on the second day of voting in the General Assembly.

I also consult Ambassador Navtej Sarna in Washington and, on his advice, decide to reach out to Ambassador Nikki Haley, the US Permanent Representative to the UN. Ever since she joined the UN, Ambassador Haley has—in personal interactions and at larger social gatherings—spoken with genuine warmth about her feelings for India. She is forthright in mentioning that she is a 'friend of India', and the 'US considers India a very important partner'. In our time of need, we sorely need some demonstration of that friendship and partnership.

As Ambassador Haley is travelling, I text her about my disappointment regarding the US mission working feverishly to get countries to change their support for India. While I understand the US is voting for the UK and acknowledge that is their sovereign choice, I convey that 'we are shocked and dismayed that the US, while proclaiming India as a strong partner, is in an unprecedented manner working to undermine our aspirations to serve on an international body'. The US mission, I complain, is actively working against our interests and disparaging us in written communications to other member states. This, to us, is difficult to comprehend as it is not in tune with our growing ties. 'All we ask is the US allow a contest on a level playing field, rather than place its considerable weight against us.'

Not long after, she responds. The US, Ambassador Haley writes, 'values its friendship with both India and the UK'. She is travelling but has immediately instructed the US mission staff to 'stand down on this' and stop any further communications to other missions on the ICJ. She acknowledges that the US should not be working against India, expresses her sadness at the developments and concludes with the hope that the work of the US mission has not significantly harmed India. Later that day, the US mission conveys to our mission's designated contact person that they have indeed acted on Ambassador Haley's instructions, following our interaction. After that, we do not come across any further information that US personnel in New York are actively working against us. It is soothing that we too have friends who matter.

Also, we insist with the presidents of both the General Assembly and the Security Council to fix a date for the next round so that there is certainty about the way forward. Several of those who are supportive of us push for an early vote and suggest that it should be no later than a week since the last vote. On the other hand, those supporting the UK are sympathetic to a 'pause'. Amidst this airing of diverse opinions, it is agreed that the next vote is to be held on Monday, 20 November, although the schedule permits holding it during the same week on Friday, 17 November. Nevertheless, there is now certainty.

Even if it is a few days later than what we prefer, this is the opportunity we are waiting for.

※

Thursday, 16 November 2017
New York

The relentless efforts we have made in anticipation of another vote are paying dividends; there is an outpouring of support from many states. Even the cautious Anjani Kumar organizes a huge social event at the UN today so that we can gather together in a visible demonstration of support before the voting on Monday, 20 November. The turnout is so vast that it boosts our morale. The contest that began as one between individual judges has metamorphosed into much more. Ambassador Inga Rhonda King, the Permanent Representative of Saint Vincent and the Grenadines, viewing the development from a Commonwealth perspective, terms it as a 'revolt of the former colonies against their former colonial master'. Others from beyond the former colonies are challenging the UK's misuse of its position on the Council to delay an early vote. All this is not without some quiet diplomacy by our energetic band of young diplomats, who are not averse to using every available trick to spread the good word around.

While we are preparing for the next round of voting, word is going around that the UK seems to be preparing a manoeuvre of its own. It is planning to stop the voting. There is talk that the UK's legal team has dug deep into its toolkit and pulled out a 'rabbit' to see itself through. All of us go on a 'rabbit hunt' to find out what is in store. The rabbit in question is the mechanism of Joint Conference, which—like several other provisions embedded into the ICJ Statue—is drawn from the ICJ's predecessor, the Permanent Court of International Justice (PCIJ) that was attached to the League of Nations from 1922 to 1946.

To us, this is both good news and bad. It means that the UK, like us, is veering towards the conclusion that seeking votes for Judge Greenwood is a lost cause. Unlike us, their path to a successful outcome is no longer premised on obtaining majority support in both bodies, but on a legal manoeuvre, using an anachronistic provision. This is worrisome. If the UK succeeds, the outcome of the decision is to be decided in the Security Council, where India has no vote and will be a bystander. The UK, which has over the years established a formidable presence as a key constituent of the Council, will be in the driver's seat. If it succeeds, its legal skills and knowledge of UN processes— honed over decades of permanent presence on the Security Council—will be difficult for us to match.

Having heard from European Union members and some others that the UK is repeatedly broaching the Joint Conference option or of sharing the seat, we have no choice but to scurry down this 'rabbit hole'. We immerse ourselves in a crash course on the issue under the tutelage of Tanmaya and Legal Adviser Umasankar, who consult extensively with UN Secretariat officials and other legal advisers.

Article 12(1) of the ICJ Statute[3] provides:

If, after the third meeting, one or more seats still remain unfilled, a Joint Conference consisting of six members, three appointed by the General Assembly and three by the Security Council, may be formed at any time at the request of either the General Assembly or the Security

Council, for the purpose of choosing by the vote of an absolute majority one name for each seat still vacant, to submit to the General Assembly and the Security Council for their respective acceptance.

This provision has never been used, ever, in the seventy-plus years of the ICJ's history to elect a judge. In the case of the PCIJ, the mechanism of the Joint Conference was used just once, in 1921, at the inception of the court, when the last of the four deputy judges was elected through a Joint Conference of the Assembly and the Council of the League. It was to ensure the completion of the court in time for the first meeting of the PCIJ in 1922.[4]

The provision was analysed by the UN Secretariat's Office of Legal Affairs in a legal opinion provided in 1984.[5] We are informed by the Secretariat officials that this still remains valid. The opinion had noted that Article 12(1) provides that a Joint Conference *may* be formed. Therefore, it was not mandatory to resort to the Joint Conference. Indeed, the opinion stated:

[S]hould a deadlock occur, a Joint Conference should not automatically be resorted to. It seems more practical that the electoral organs should proceed to further 'meetings'.

Resorting to a Joint Conference will mean a transfer of power from both the bodies of the UN to a select group. Consequently, there is an unwillingness amongst the general membership of the General Assembly and the Security Council to resort to it. Hence, they had in the past always followed the advice of the Office of Legal Affairs to proceed with further meetings to vote for the judges.

The opinion also notes that the ICJ Statute is explicit in requiring an absolute majority of both organs in the case of elections to the ICJ. Usually this means eight votes (and not nine as required for other Council decisions) are needed in the Council and there are no vetoes. However, a decision about setting up a Joint Conference is a procedural one of the Council and requires nine affirmative votes and is not subject to a veto.

The more we delve into the implications, the greater the number of unforeseen issues that surface if the Joint Conference is agreed to by a decision of the Security Council. It will open a new can of worms on matters, ranging from the criteria of selection of its members, the modalities for the conduct of work and the process of acceptance of the outcome. For example, there is no clarity on how each of the bodies will select three members each to be part of the Joint Conference. Whether they will consult each other or decide by themselves is an open issue, as is whether regional diversity and gender equality will be factors or not. Since any recommendation will need to be decided by a majority of four, what will happen in case such majority cannot be arrived at? Will this trigger the never-used mechanism in Article 12(3) of the ICJ Statute[6] which provides for the ICJ judges to decide on the matter. Also, even if there is a positive recommendation of the Joint Conference, it has to be accepted by both the organs. What if one or the other organ does not accept the proposal, especially since the Joint Conference is not constrained to make its choice from amongst those who were nominated within the time frame provided in the initial notification of the vacancies? In 1921, the deputy judge recommended and finally appointed to the PCIJ was not amongst the contenders who were voted for by either of the two bodies.

The UK is planning to use its privileged perch on the Council to get a decision that will take the entire UN membership into uncharted territory. It is opting against an option that the UN Secretariat suggests is more practical. It is trying in the twenty-first century to resort to a tool that has been used only once in the twentieth century and that too ninety-six years ago. All this means it is not an appetizing option for us. We also feel that it will not appeal to the overwhelming majority of the UN membership. However, the UK is not interested in the views of the entire membership. All it requires is eight members of the Security Council to join in support. It is shifting the contest to a new battlefield and is gambling that it will score there. While we are confident that we are on the verge of scoring big on the field that we were playing for so long, the UK is bent on not only shifting the goal posts but trying to change the game itself.

After carefully considering every aspect, we decide that not only can we not support this, but we need to actively oppose it, since this is the UK's way of undermining our imminent success. However, opposition to the proposition means that we now have to add another layer to our campaign and sensitize countries to the implications of the UK's move and seek their support to oppose it. This is in addition to seeking their vote for Judge Bhandari, which we cannot give up pursuing as that is the basis of our core strength.

In the digital era, it is not a tough task to point out the pitfalls of the UK proposal to UN delegates. We have a system of reaching out at three levels in every mission. We activate that with a one-page note that explains, in a lucid manner, the complex problems the UK's proposal will lead to, with no oversight from any UN body. In addition, at the request of the ambassador of Bolivia, I brief the elected members at an informal meeting convened in the anteroom of the Council. I also reach out to the rest of the permanent members individually.

The more difficult task is to get senior leaders of countries in the Security Council to comprehend and support our objections on such a 'technical' matter. We are now required to ask for additional support beyond a vote for an Indian judge. We are to ask for the process as it has been envisaged thus far to continue, rather than allowing it to be changed. Also, since time is of the essence, we cannot wait for the UK to formally make the proposal before engaging at senior levels.

At no stage did Ambassador Matthew Rycroft ever discuss the issue of the Joint Conference with me on the 'private line' until now, when he brings the matter up in the informal consultations of the Council. He gives notice that the UK will seek a decision by the Council on 20 November, the day of the voting. This is by way of informing delegations to seek instructions when the matter comes up. Only after that does he call and inform me about it. Obviously, it is not a conversation that leaves either of us in a happy state of mind. It is clear that the die, so to say, is cast.

Friday, 17 November 2017
New York

Well-disposed Security Council ambassadors share their assessments that all members do not want to show their cards. Several who support us raise questions and objections. The UK's position is that it is a legally valid choice and will provide a way out of the stalemate. A couple of UK supporters are vociferous in their advocacy of the solution. Some say that there appear to be differences on the issue, but nothing more. Many keep silent. The UK, by its subsequent actions, seems to conclude that the numbers are in its favour as the majority has not objected.

Those who provide us readouts of the informal consultations counsel that now is the time to undertake whatever heavy-lifting we can do. I call Foreign Secretary Dr Jaishankar after the UK's move and convey this. I explain that I have reached out to all the other permanent members individually, and none has provided any comfort beyond giving me a patient hearing. However, all of them have mentioned that, as yet, they are awaiting instructions and have left me with some slender hope.

France, in particular, seems to have even bought into the UK's argument. Their suave Permanent Representative, Ambassador François Delattre, is the longest serving ambassador amongst those from the permanent members. In response to my plea for support, he responds that he is 'unaware of Indian objections'. He then explains in some detail that he views the proposal as a sophisticated way out for the 'two giants' involved in this major clash, as none wanted to give way otherwise. I vent all this to Dr Jaishankar. He hears me out. He says that the matter had come up in the meeting that Prime Minister Modi had with Foreign Minister Jean-Yves Le Drian of France, who was in New Delhi on a two-day visit. Minister Le Drian had explained France's repeated votes for the UK. However, he has given his solemn commitment that France will not agree to stop the voting as being proposed by the UK but will support India's stance on not delaying the vote by opting for a Joint Conference. Dr Jaishankar says that I should leave the matter with him as the visiting minister is still in Delhi. Late evening, I receive confirmation in New York that following our discussions earlier, 'Paris was consulted and they have agreed to our request that the vote should proceed on Monday, without disruption'. It means there is substantial accretion in our camp on the procedural matter.

⸰⸰⸰

Saturday, 18 November 2017
New York

Weekends are usually when UN diplomacy takes a break. Many diplomats guard their time away from work zealously. Some even decline to respond to any messages over the weekend. For a few, weekends are invariably sacrosanct. This weekend, Indian diplomats are breaking all these well-understood practices. Each of us is persistently trying to engage with our interlocutors, pass on relevant information and seek confirmation of support or clarity of their stance.

Never before have I sent so many individual messages to each of my peers as I do this weekend. It is the same with each of the other diplomats at the mission. We work, as usual, but from home—except for the mandatory two meetings at the beginning and end of the day in the office. We are bolstered by the arrival of two more officers, Counsellor Devesh Uttam and Counsellor Manjunath, who hit the ground running. Having served in New York until less than a year earlier, they have their contacts in various missions and are engaged with them over the weekend. The Asia–Europe Meeting (ASEM) at the foreign ministers' level is scheduled on 20–21 November in Nay Pyi Taw, Myanmar, and Minister of State General V.K. Singh plans to meet several key players there. Secretary (East) Preeti Saran and our ambassador in Myanmar, Vikram Misri, are engaging senior officials who have reached there ahead of the meeting. The difference in time zones helps us keep the momentum on a twenty-four-hour basis.

In all this activity, I have been remiss and have flouted a key principle of diplomatic protocol. While I had hosted Judge Bhandari and his wife, Madhu Bhandari, at various receptions and we conversed regularly, I realize that I am guilty of not inviting them over for a meal. This weekend is the only opportunity to correct this failing. We decide to meet over lunch. I request Tanmaya and his wife, Sumita, to join us too.

The diligent pursuit of official objectives is normal in any profession. As diplomats, there is a tendency for our families too to get immersed deeply in sharing the burden, even if vicariously at times. My near obsession with the ICJ means that my wife, Padma, can't remain oblivious. Having followed the process, she has always been expressing the opinion that both the Asian candidates will win. This is not the conventional wisdom that prevails amongst the more knowledgeable. Nevertheless, both of us are now confident of Judge Bhandari's victory. On the other hand, Judge Bhandari is less certain, while Madhu Bhandari, who is a lawyer herself, is more hopeful. Tanmaya, as usual, is cautious; Sumita is more optimistic. In a relaxed atmosphere, we chat about everything and anything, enjoying the south Indian *thali* prepared by Padma in deference to Judge Bhandari and Madhu Bhandari's dietary preferences.

'It is enough. All of you have done your very best. This has been an exceptional effort. Way beyond what I ever thought possible. Let us leave it at that,' Judge Bhandari vents his feelings. Having been through the nerve-wracking experience over so many days with quiet dignity, he is now ready to graciously give in. He is reflecting the same feeling of bringing closure to the subject that many others have voiced. However, hearing it from the candidate himself is quite a jolt for me. As part of our effort to keep him above the fray, we are not filling him in with all the details. At the reception for election officers arranged by Anjani Kumar on the UN premises over the prior weekend, Judge Bhandari met the huge number of delegates who had poured in to greet him and provide reassurance of their support. However, he did not make any stump speech, as it would, of necessity, have to touch on various political issues. Instead, I spoke at some length and dwelt on the issues at stake and sought the support of the large gathering.

I now take the opportunity to explain to Judge Bhandari, in great detail, the enormity of the efforts being undertaken globally and counsel patience. It is not an individual's fight. 'It is also no longer a fight that we can walk away from, or afford to lose,' I argue. We have put in all that we can and then some more. This has been an unparalleled election in the annals of Indian diplomacy. The decisive phase is beckoning. All of us need to keep the faith. We need to hold our nerve. I tell him of the pulls and pressures where some want a compromise and are ready for a negotiated outcome. However, we have resisted all this in the belief that we will prevail.

Judge Bhandari listens patiently, nods and then cryptically remarks, 'I understand the enormity of the pressure better now. I realize why Judge Greenwood is leaving over the weekend and is not going to be present at the General Assembly Hall on Monday, 20 November.' While I do not probe him on what he means by that, to me it confirms that the UK is no longer in it for the election. The UK is now going to put all it has into the move to stall the election. We, therefore, need to ensure that, as a priority, we stop that endeavour. Everything else is secondary.

—⊶⊷—

Sunday, 19 November 2017
New York

Sections of the Indian media are now following the issue closely. Some are highlighting the UK's effort as tactics reminiscent of the robber baron Robert Clive.[7] The mood of the media, as of officialdom in India, is turning dark. The twists and turns are taking their toll. Multilateral elections are usually insulated from the public glare and do not engender much interest. This is turning out to be different.

The two big election results at the UN that are etched in the memory of many are both where India had been bested. In October 1975, India had withdrawn from the contest for a non-permanent seat on the Security Council prior to the eighth round on day three, after having trailed for six of the seven previous rounds of voting spread over two consecutive days.[8] In 1996, in the election for a non-permanent seat on the Security Council, India had lost to Japan by a huge margin in just one round.[9] The only other UN election that had engendered public interest in India had been Dr Shashi Tharoor's bid to become the Secretary General in 2007. That attempt too was given up after several 'straw polls' indicated that one of the P-5 was discouraging Dr Tharoor's candidacy. It is for the first time that a significant global election is moving in a favourable direction for India.

Every diplomatic challenge always throws up opportunities. It is only a matter of finding them. Usually, we tend to miss the opportunities and get overwhelmed by the challenge. While we were seeing the election as an unprecedented diplomatic opportunity, others were seeing it as a portent of the decline of Indian diplomacy. Some ill-informed commentators on social media are harping on about how India, having lost to Lebanon, is continuing to battle on in a lost cause. It shows a lack of understanding of the process. How does one lose a multi-seat election when one seat is still to be decided? Even if, for the sake of argument, that is taken as correct, who did the UK lose to so as to be in the contest with India? Was it Somalia that had bested the UK?

Then there are other experts who are putting forth the view that the allocated Asia-Pacific seat has already been filled. If that is so, why is India—an Asia-Pacific member—being allowed to contest a seat that is not available for it? If the seat is for West Europe, why is the UK not objecting to India contesting it? But then, neither the traditional media nor social media are places to settle such issues or to exorcise the ghosts of the past. We decide that we need to keep our poise and focus on what we have to do on the UN platform rather than on digital or media platforms.

Meanwhile, the President of the General Assembly announces that he will make a last-ditch effort to seek a mutually acceptable outcome and wants the principals alone to attend a meeting that he will convene at noon on 20 November, the day of the third round of voting. We need to prepare ourselves both for the voting as well as the negotiations before the voting.

10

Please Don't Pick Up
the Phone

—∞∞∞—

Monday, 20 November 2017
New York

DIPLOMATS, BY TRADITION and inclination, are practitioners of the art of finding pathways out of difficult situations. In multilateral institutions, often this quest reflects in the search for what are termed as 'win-win' outcomes. Such is the wide acceptance of the mantra of 'win-win' that any unwillingness to conform to it is viewed as a deviation from the pursuit of the common good. In multilateral formats, where diverse interests are involved and an array of stakeholders require their objectives to be met, anyone seeking a derogation from the favoured model of 'win-win' solutions is viewed as a stick in the mud, out to undermine the spirit of multilateralism.

Since negotiations are the principal tool available to multilateral diplomats, 'give and take' negotiations leading to a 'compromise' are the Holy Grail. In many instances, compromises suit everyone's interests. However, this need not be so in all cases. Such situations always pose a dilemma for those pursuing key national interests in multilateral settings. We are confronted with this conundrum as we prepare for the crucial negotiations that the President of the General Assembly has convened on the way forward. We need to ensure a balance in abiding by the 'mood music' of multilateral negotiations, without underplaying our hand and frittering away the advantage we have established on the ground in the pursuit of an important goal.

We are way ahead in the electoral arena. All indications, gleaned from inputs received from colleagues from every part of the world, are that if the voting is held for the entire session of three hours, we will overwhelm the United Kingdom in the General Assembly. If there are to be five votes, like there were on the second day of voting, it will mean that in more than ten consecutive direct votes the Indian candidate will have scored hugely over the UK candidate. We estimate that our votes are likely to swell to between 135 to 140 by the end of the day. It will be well above the two-thirds majority of the entire membership. No candidate who has ever lost the confidence of such a huge majority can still lay claim to being a judge on the world court.

Our interest does not, therefore, lie in agreeing to a compromise solution at this stage. We are entering into a phase which plays to our strength. What is the need to compromise before the vote? If required, a compromise can be worked on later. That option can be considered if our projections fail to materialize. Even then, the enhancing of the lead will leave us in a much better position to negotiate on the day after, rather than before, the third day of voting.

What we need to do is to find ways of addressing any compromise only after the vote. It requires us to marshal facts and figures that can be presented as reasoned justification for the voting to take place. Lakshmi Swaminathan, who has by now got used to ferreting out nuggets of information from historical records, is tasked again to look at all elections of the past and make a comparative analysis. While she has projected that we can reach our target of two-thirds majority in a couple of rounds, for us it is now important to look up how much longer it has taken others to reach victory in the past. The idea is to see if we can string together coherent arguments that can indicate that compromises were not resorted to in similar situations in the past and hence it is too early to do so now.

Arguments, facts, and figures—however valid and irrefutable—are only one aspect of negotiations. They are never adequate by themselves to achieve objectives during negotiations. Many diplomats tend to overestimate the power of logic in inter-state discussions. Negotiations are different from seminars and symposia. Intellectual arguments are essential prerequisites, but they need to be backed up with a sound assessment of 'ground realities'. Battles won on the field are rarely lost on the negotiating table. In multilateral settings, additionally, confidence about support from other stakeholders for the stance that is adopted is a bonus. Shrewd negotiators tend to bulldoze their way through. Hence, there needs to be more in the arsenal than arguments to make them back off.

In planning for the negotiations, it is apparent that we may have the arguments but do not, as yet, have enough support for our objective of continuing the election process so as to deter the UK from any precipitate action. We need more support in the Security Council. That is the key ingredient in determining whether we will succeed in stopping the UK from bringing the process to a halt. It is a tough ask to take on a permanent member in its den. The UK is aware of this overwhelming advantage it has. Hence, it is intent on proceeding with the effort to call for a vote on the Joint Conference, invoking an anachronistic clause which has not been used in the UN before. Legally, it is well within its rights to do so, even though the publicly articulated advice of the UN legal office is not in support. Morally, it will be seen as a dubious move. It is apparent that in circumstances where its candidate is being routed in the General Assembly, a state is using its privileged position in the Security Council to bring that vote to a stop. The UK seems to have calculated that it is a price worth paying. We decide that we need to try and raise that price much higher.

The UK is banking on all its eight other supporters in the secret balloting standing up along with it in the open and showing their hand in favour of the Joint Conference in a recorded procedural vote in the Council. That is all it needs. That was its assessment of the state of affairs when it proceeded to inform Council members on 16 November of its intent.

We need to get more support. Following the reply from France, I get the much-awaited responses from the other permanent members. As Ambassador Haley is travelling, I had sent her an email listing out the adverse impact of making a move on the Joint Conference as it could have unforeseen implications. As she is aware of the 'private line', I mention that such a peremptory move will reduce space for negotiations, if they are required, in case the stalemate continues. Besides, in the wider world and in India, the view will be that the move is an effort to stop a democratic exercise of voting. This will not be helpful to a solution. Since it is the weekend, the wait for me seems interminable. With less than twenty-four hours to go, I receive a response. It is short but meets our needs. It confirms that the US supports waiting to have the vote the next day and ends with wishing us luck.

We have a few hours more. External Affairs Minister Sushma Swaraj is to talk to Wang Yi and Sergei Lavrov, the foreign ministers of China and Russia respectively. The telephone call with the Chinese foreign minister is not scheduled as his office mentions that he is travelling and unable to take the call. Swaraj says she had a 'good' conversation with Minister Lavrov. 'He understands all the nuances of the Security Council procedures,' she says, adding that he has served as the Russian ambassador at the UN for nearly a decade before he was elevated to foreign minister in 2004. She suggests that I follow up the conversation in New York with their ambassador.

—❦—

Early in the morning, we are told that the Russian Permanent Representative, Ambassador Vasily Nebenzya, will meet me at 11.30 a.m. in the Delegates Lounge. Ambassador Nebenzya has worked on multilateral issues for many years and has served in New York earlier. He joined as Permanent Representative only at the end of July, following the sudden death of his predecessor, Ambassador Vitali Churkin, who had served for more than a decade at the UN. During my earlier interactions with him, he was cautious but always understanding and considerate to our points of view. I promptly agree to meet him as per his convenience. The location and the timing are just right. It means that before going into the negotiations, I will have the responses of all permanent members—bar China. I have already discarded any possibility of a response from the Chinese Charge d'Affaires a.i.

Lakshmi, who has been burrowing through Security Council documentation, summarizes the outcome of her research about past Security Council practice. The piece of paper is the only thing I carry with me. It has several numbers, each of which can be elaborated into arguments.

One final task remains. At 11 a.m., I have a telephonic conference to seek final instructions before departing for the United Nations. 'We are all together and have had an initial discussion about your suggestions,' begins Dr Jaishankar. It is 8.30 p.m. in New Delhi. I picture the brain's trust of the Ministry of External Affairs converging together at the External Affairs Minister's residence in the familiar meeting room. Minister of State M.J. Akbar as well as all the secretaries of the ministry then in Delhi are present.

Rather than asking me to repeat my assessment, Dr Jaishankar summarizes my understanding of the situation and asks me to add anything else that I want after that. He begins, 'According to you, our vote tally in the General Assembly will surge today. Your estimation is that we will reach and go beyond the two-thirds majority of the entire membership of the UN. Then, you believe that it will not be sustainable for the UK's candidate to continue. So, your recommendation is that we are in striking distance and, therefore, should not at this stage agree to any deal—whatever its contours.'

There was little else to add to that summation. I affirm after each of the points he makes. At the end, I mention that we also seem to be in a good position in terms of the votes required in the Security Council to stall the UK's move there to invoke the Joint Conference option. 'The UK's belief that all the nine who support Judge Greenwood will also stand in their corner to block further voting and transfer the issue to the Joint Conference is coming apart.' Already, 'thanks to high-level intervention in Delhi, France has shown reluctance to support the UK on that'. I then raise a few issues. Will the UK want to proceed in light of the lack of P-5 unity? The US position on this seems also supportive of us, although it was not clear if the US will be in favour of an entire session of voting or be satisfied with a few more ballots. Also, two of the ten non-permanent members among the nine voting for the UK are always telling us that they are voting for us. Will both of them want it to be made known to us publicly that while they have consistently assured us of support, they have in secret ballots voted constantly for the UK? We still are awaiting Russia's response. All this means that the UK is on a shaky wicket, and we must stay away from any talk of a solution other than a full session of voting today.

External Affairs Minister Sushma Swaraj has the last word. She recalls that they had a fairly long and robust discussion on all aspects that have been mentioned. They understood the rationale of the recommendations made. Thus far, they have gone by the assessments and proposals being made by the mission in New York to the ministry. On this occasion too, they are going by the recommendations made. She concludes by wishing all of us luck and hopes for a good outcome at the negotiations and in the voting.

Reinforcement of a plan of action proposed from the field by those who matter at the headquarters invariably adds immensely to the confidence of those on the ground. The entire conversation lasts about twenty minutes. However, the go-ahead from the Ministry of External Affairs top leadership means the world to all of us in New York. I quickly share this with Tanmaya. He, in turn, communicates to all the others the gist, appropriately, as it is important for all of us to be on the same page at this final juncture.

The explicit support has stiffened my backbone. If, as the joke goes, 'every year in service, you tend to lose a vertebra' is the touchstone, I have lost all of my vertebrae. The reassurances during the phone call are a booster dose of confidence as I set forth to the UN premises.

The lounge is full of delegates. Several are aware of the impending voting and wish me well. As soon as I take my seat, Ambassador Nebenzya comes over, accompanied by a colleague. 'What is your scenario?' he asks, seeking a quick assessment of what the sequence playing out today will be. He acknowledges that we will gain votes in the balloting. Then he adds that 'despite the excellent ties that exist between our two countries—which are much better than the ties between Russia and UK—we are bound by the unwritten but long-standing understanding of exchange of votes by the permanent members for their respective candidates whenever elections are held in the Security Council.' In light of that, he affirms that they cannot deviate from their support for Judge Greenwood.

I remind him about the 'good' telephone conversation that the two ministers had. Ambassador Nebenzya says he has seen the readout. He has received directions that they will not have any objections to our insistence that the voting should continue for a session today. 'Close it today. Tomorrow, it may be different. I wish you luck,' he ends the conversation. It is all I need.

Counsellor Anjani Kumar comes rushing to me. He has just heard from the office of the President of the General Assembly that one more delegate can accompany each of the ambassadors at the meeting. I would dearly have wanted the calm presence of Tanmaya or our legal adviser. It is too late now as we only have a few minutes before the meeting. Anyhow, legal nuances perhaps don't matter any more. I am certain the UK does not have the nine votes to stop the voting today.

—⁂—

The small meeting room in the General Assembly President's chambers is overflowing. Looking around, I realize my folly in not asking someone—anyone—to join me. The President of the General Assembly, Foreign Minister of the Slovak Republic Miroslav Lajčák, is already present. He is accompanied by his Chef de Cabinet, Ambassador František Ružička, who served for five years as the Slovak Permanent Representative to the UN before changing his role to assist his minister. Ambassador Sebastiano Cardi, the Italian Permanent Representative who is the President of the Security Council for November, comes in with his Political Coordinator for Security Council matters. Ambassador Rycroft joins with his legal adviser. Also present are the legal adviser to the President of the General Assembly and some UN Secretariat officials.

Following the exchange of courtesies, President Lajčák begins the discussions: 'After consultations with the President of the Council, I have convened this meeting to try and see if there are ways to amicably address issues pertaining to the ICJ elections.' He then asks the main protagonists to put forth their perspectives. Ambassador Rycroft starts, 'In the election underway, despite many rounds of balloting, there is a deadlock in filling the fifth position of the judge of the ICJ. The UK feels this is an appropriate case to invoke Article 12 of the ICJ Statute. It proposes to follow the procedure and request a decision by the Security Council after one more round of voting in the afternoon.' He then adds, 'We would have preferred to invoke it before the voting begins but, in deference to some suggestions, we are ready to wait for a single round of voting before proceeding.'

In response, I take out the paper containing the figures that have been painstakingly researched by Lakshmi. I acknowledge that legally there is no bar to resorting to the Joint Conference as is being proposed by the UK. However, the seventy-year history of the UN has provided some pointers to the established practice in such cases. Never has the Joint Conference mechanism been resorted to, even though there were numerous cases where the elections were spread over a longer period in terms of number of days, number of meetings and number of rounds of balloting. I then provide a series of examples:

- In 1956, the election process to fill a single vacancy was stretched to over six months and spread to the next year when the composition of the Council's membership was changed. The process which began in June 1956 was only completed in January 1957.[1]
- In 1966, there were twenty meetings before the elections could be completed.[2] In 1978, the Security Council had voted fourteen times before the election was completed.[3]
- In 2011, the elections were spread over more than a month from 10 November to 13 December.[4]
- In 2014, there were fifteen rounds of votes in the General Assembly and eleven in the Security Council.[5]

In none of the cases had there been a resort to the Joint Conference. Yet, now, when neither the number of days nor the number of meetings or the number of ballots has exceeded these past examples, we are being asked to follow a route that has never been followed in the past. I end by suggesting that the Secretariat officials present can be asked to check the veracity of the facts and indicate why in each case the Joint Conference was not opted for and what is unique now.

I can see the Secretariat officials confer and prepare to respond. However, Ambassador Rycroft swiftly intervenes before anyone can take up the suggestion I made. 'The proposal that the UK is putting forth is legally sound and even India acknowledges this,' he emphasizes. Then he adds, 'It does not require to be checked against past practice. That it was not pursued in the past does not mean it should not be followed now.' He haughtily dismisses the various examples I have provided by saying, 'Different things are done at different times.' These are all political decisions made by following the procedures laid down, he suggests, adding that the UK has already broached the issue amongst Council members and is now ready to proceed, after the first round.

Ambassador Cardi, who had been previously indicating that Italy is not comfortable with adopting the procedure, intervenes to add, 'My assessment is that the Council members will be ready to decide on the matter, if it is taken up after the first round of balloting.'

President Lajčák joins in. 'I have consulted the UN Secretariat. The General Assembly will have to halt the balloting after the first round if the Security Council is going to discuss the Joint Conference issue after the first round in the afternoon. The balloting has to proceed independently and simultaneously in both the main organs. If one body cannot do so and is considering alternative legal options that are available, the General Assembly too would have to wait for that outcome.'

He suggests that it will be more appropriate if the meeting can agree on a common path forward.

It seems to me that a triple team is in the making. The UK is being facilitated in their assertion to move ahead. It is time to go on the offensive. I shift to the procedural track and explain: In the past, India has never objected to the process being followed. We did not object when the second day of voting was shifted from the announced date of 10 November to 13 November without consulting us. We never queried when only five rounds of balloting were held on 13 November, although in the last such instance the balloting lasted for seven rounds. On 17 November, there were no meetings scheduled in the Council and the General Assembly, yet the request to have the balloting on that day was not agreed to, and instead both the presiding officers in their wisdom had decided on 20 November. Yet now, a few hours before the time fixed by the two Presidents for an entire session of voting, we are being told by both of them that there can be only one round of balloting and nothing more.

My argument seems to have hit where it hurt. The alibis roll out quickly. Ambassador Cardi says, 'The Security Council was ready on the 11th for balloting, and it was not on account of them that the vote could not be held.' Ambassador Ružička responds, 'We were ready to continue to vote on the 13th, but it was on account of other commitments of the President of the Council…' None addressed the issue of why the voting was not held on 17 November.

President Lajčák realizes that raking up process-oriented differences of the past is sowing disarray. He deftly veers the discussion back to the way forward and suggests a 'compromise'. He proposes 'a suggestion that perhaps all can agree' on: 'Three rounds of balloting can be held before the UK seeks recourse to the Joint Conference.' Ambassador Cardi quickly seconds it as a 'reasonable' approach and urges acceptance.

For a moment, I too am taken in. It can work for us, I think. We will, in the space of three rounds, most likely, get to the requisite majority. However, it also strikes me that if we agree to this and do not get to a huge majority, the UK will have the option of suggesting the Joint Conference to the exclusion of any other option that we think fit to break the deadlock. Also, if everyone knew that is the path we have agreed to in advance, it will be seen as a 'back room' deal and a 'let down' by some. In any case, by our calculations, the UK does not have the requisite support to get their proposal accepted in the Council today if we oppose it. Why then do we need to give in when we hold all the cards?

By my reckoning, two people in the room know that the UK cannot proceed without our acceptance—Ambassador Rycroft and I. The rest are bystanders with little at stake. Ambassador Rycroft, I am sure, has been sensitized by some of the other permanent members who were not on board on the Joint Conference proposal being put to vote today. As Lord Ahmad candidly acknowledges later in a submission to the House of Commons Foreign Affairs Committee:[6] 'We certainly took soundings from some of the P-5 members in the context of the Security Council, and it was our view that support for the mechanism would not be supported by others.'

Ambassador Rycroft is, therefore, hoping that this meeting will get us on board in some manner or the other. Only then can he proceed on the Joint Conference path. Otherwise he cannot and will not do so. A permanent member will not risk a loss of its proposal to invoke the Joint Conference in the

Security Council on account of opposition from a non-member of the Council. On the other hand, they are also aware that five ballots will certainly expose the huge decline in support and leave a devastating impact. In accordance with our plans, this is no time to offer the UK the path that it hopes to get from the meeting.

I thank President Lajčák for the proposal but say, 'We fail to understand why the effort is on to shorten the scheduled number of votes.' Then I add, 'We are confident that at the end of the day we will win. If the UK thinks otherwise, the balloting will decide that. We are ready to negotiate tomorrow, if the outcome is not decisively settled today. However, we are confident it will be over today.'

Elaborating this line of thinking, I add, 'What difference will two more rounds of balloting make for the UK, if it is certain that the deadlock will continue? There is no tearing hurry to choose an option today, before there can be serious consultations amongst our capitals in keeping with the excellent bilateral ties we have.' I acknowledge, 'In the middle of a vigorous campaign, I may not be the best person to negotiate. So, we will be willing to negotiate anywhere the UK chooses. In London, if it wants... High Commissioner Yash Sinha could be engaged, or in New Delhi, if the UK so chooses to designate High Commissioner Sir Dominic Asquith.' However, 'If the UK peremptorily tries today to resort to an option it has chosen of its own volition, despite our clearly voiced concerns, then everything is going to be off the table,' I warn. The UK and those who want to go ahead, rejecting our offer to negotiate with serious intent tomorrow, will be responsible for what will follow, both in terms of our rallying against the Joint Conference option in the Security Council and the uproar many in the General Assembly will raise, as they will view it as a purposeful bid to undermine the General Assembly by the Security Council without any consultations.' I conclude that in this case, 'What may be legally permissible is not politically wise and diplomatically sagacious.'

With this I signal that I have other commitments and have to leave. Everyone realizes that the meeting is ending where it began. There is no progress. The last hope for a 'compromise' has passed. The UK now has hard choices to make. They can allow the balloting and lose the election, or they can try to activate the Joint Conference and lose the procedural vote on that.

'It was a tough meeting, but I think we were able to hold our nerve,' I later tell Dr Jaishankar. I also update him on the Russian response and express confidence that we are on good ground. Following our conversation, he texts, 'Datte raho' (Stay the course).

I head to a luncheon meeting hosted by my long-time friend, Ambassador Mansour Al Otaibi. He has invited a large number of Permanent Representatives to seek their inputs, as Kuwait is preparing to enter the Security Council as a non-permanent member in 2018-19. Ordinarily, I would not have joined the occasion just ahead of the vote. Ambassador Otaibi, however, promises that I can make a sales pitch for votes and leave soon after. It is a good offer that I cannot afford to decline in my circumstances. Even as I am speaking, I hear the sounds of several texts. As soon as I finish, I rummage through the text messages and see one from Dr Jaishankar that says that Foreign Secretary Boris Johnson of the UK is trying to contact the External Affairs Minister in New Delhi.

I do not even see the rest of his messages; I take leave of the host and hurriedly call Dr Jaishankar. Before hearing me out, he assures me, 'Relax, we know your views.' Nevertheless, I urge, 'Please don't put him through.' In the midst of the battle, all I am thinking is that there may be some offer that the UK may make that would be difficult for the minister to decline. So single-minded am I in denying an exit route to the UK that it never occurs to me that the UK may be seeking to contact the minister for anything else.

My thoughts drift back to the warm initial meeting between Boris Johnson and Sushma Swaraj at a reception hosted during the General Assembly session in New York a few months ago, at the end of September. Foreign Secretary Johnson had reacted with enthusiasm as I introduced Minister Swaraj to him. Shaking his head several times, he had muttered, 'Sushma, oh Sushma,' and then excitedly grabbed her hand, pivoting towards the next room to tell Prime Minister Theresa May with great relish that 'Sushma has come'. The reception had clashed with the annual US reception by President Donald Trump, and Minister Swaraj had indeed made the extra effort to attend the UK reception.

These thoughts make my concerns mount about what may happen now if they talk. To assuage my anxiety, I decide to call the minister's residence. It is already late but, having worked with her for long in Delhi and in my present assignment, I know she will understand.

'Ma'am, please don't pick up the phone,' I plead.

She laughs disarmingly and replies, 'I have listened to you all the time.'

I complete the conversation and head to the UN. Along the way, I see I have two missed calls from Ambassador Rycroft.

Many concerns are flooding in. I think it best to just wait for some time rather than call back immediately. A few minutes later, I am at the UN gate. There is still more than an hour before the vote. The phone buzzes again.

This is Dr Jaishankar. 'We've done it!' he exclaims. 'I just got a message that the UK is withdrawing its candidate,' he adds.

Overjoyed, I do not even ask who has communicated the message. 'I am ready for retirement,' I say out of sheer relief.

For me, the feeling that the saga is over is overwhelming. I tell him that following our earlier conversation I had not responded to the UK Permanent Representative's missed call and will do so now to get confirmation.

Shortly thereafter, Ambassador Rycroft confirms that they have consulted Judge Greenwood and will withdraw his candidature. He congratulates me and mentions that they will take some time to formally convey this to the two presiding officers. I thank him for their graciousness and assure him that we will leave it to them to communicate to all concerned in any manner they consider appropriate. Over the next hour, the UK conveys its decision to various interlocutors. All that is left is to accept the felicitations, join in the celebrations and complete the formalities of the official voting in both the organs.

Judge Bhandari, the only candidate left in the contest, secures all fifteen votes in the Security Council and 183 in the General Assembly.

Epilogue

Where Interests Coincide, Everything Is Kept Aside

NATIONAL ELECTIONS ARE often a metaphor for change. In the international arena, this is rarely so. While many reasons account for this, it is primarily because the nature of contestation is fundamentally different. In democracies, elections represent opportunities for change. The international system is rigid and elections rarely reflect fundamental change. Also, elections on global platforms rarely attract much interest beyond the diplomatic fraternity. The outcome of the voting at the United Nations for the ICJ election on 20 November 2017 was different.

It was diplomacy and not international law that decided the outcome. This has always been the case. The only difference was that the UK and its allies in the Security Council have traditionally been the beneficiaries of the established dispensation of geopolitical forces behind the curtain of international justice. This time, the changes in the changing global dispensation attracted attention.

Oliver Wright, writing in the London-based daily *The Times*, reported that Britain had lost out under the 'new world order' at the United Nations, blaming a 'rebellion' by 'an alliance of developing nations'. The result, it noted, meant cracking open a club that for decades now had taken it for granted that the five permanent members of the UN Security Council would always have a seat at the ICJ.[1]

Owen Bowcott, writing in *The Guardian*, termed it as 'a humiliating blow to British international prestige and an acceptance of a diminished status in international affairs'.[2]

The BBC's diplomatic correspondent wrote, 'This defeat at the UN will be seen as a significant diplomatic setback, a symbol of Britain's reduced status on the world stage. Britain tried to win an election—but the community of nations backed the other side.'[3]

Later, following a post-mortem of the episode, the UK's Foreign Affairs Committee concluded:[4] 'The inability of the government to secure the re-election of Sir Christopher Greenwood to the court was a failure of UK diplomacy.'

In India, on the night of the election, External Affairs Minister Sushma Swaraj did not sleep much. She kept track of the voting on the UN's Web TV Livestream and seemed to have savoured it all. As soon as the formal announcements ended the meetings in the Security Council and the General Assembly, she called and congratulated the entire team in New York. In her own words, she saw it as 'akin to being engaged in a second war of Independence'.

Vijay Gokhale, who went on to succeed Dr Jaishankar as Foreign Secretary, in a tribute to Sushma Swaraj on her death anniversary recounted, 'She phoned each of the senior officials in New Delhi and personally conveyed the news while thanking them for their efforts. Not only did she lead from the front but also ended the saga with a graciousness that will be remembered for long by all who were engaged in it.'[5]

The print and the visual media in India carried reports of the 'diplomatic coup'.[6] The outcome was not perceived as a contest between two individuals or judicial philosophies, but between the old post-World War II order and the emerging dynamics of world power.[7]

Social media was agog with the who's who of India's political firmament, including Prime Minister Narendra Modi, showering accolades on the diplomatic establishment.[8] In keeping with the mood of national euphoria, commentators termed it as a 'power shift' attributable to 'smart and aggressive diplomacy', reflecting a 'hunger that was absent before'.[9]

At one level, legal analysts projected the result as 'an important departure from ICJ election practice'. They said, 'First, it did away with the tradition that reserved a seat on the court for the five permanent members of the Security Council. Second, it was noteworthy because it resulted in a reallocation of seats amongst the regional groups.'[10] Whether this was on account of Indian exceptionalism, and if it set a trend for the future, can only be fully understood following subsequent ICJ election results.

At another level, the argument made was that it showed that India had 'an abiding interest in international regimes that were set up after World War II, believing their stability is crucial to India's rise'. Therefore, 'in an age of revisionism and aggressive lawfare led by China, India's election to the ICJ is likely a stabilizing development'.[11]

On 17 July 2019, the ICJ delivered its final verdict on the Kulbhushan Jadhav case between India and Pakistan. By a 15:1 majority decision in India's favour, the court found that Pakistan had breached its obligations under the 1963 Vienna Convention on Consular Relations and called for an effective review and reconsideration of the conviction and sentence of Kulbhushan Jadhav.[12] Notwithstanding the outcome at the ICJ, the question of Kulbhushan Jadhav's detention and his pending death sentence remains, until now, caught up in the perennial uncertainty that pervades bilateral ties between India and Pakistan.

The election also symbolized the coming-of-age of Indian multilateral diplomacy. The lessons we learnt were many. Our decision-making process may, at times, be time-consuming and can put a heavy load on ensuring the implementation of a decision that has taken a long time to arrive at in the first place. However, once a decision is taken, with all on board, the trajectory is never half-hearted. It usually proceeds at full throttle to achieve success. Focus provided by the political leadership sets the tone for the rest.

A headquarter-driven approach is required to pursue ambitious goals globally. On its own, a single diplomatic mission cannot succeed in the pursuit of major goals, as every aspect of a country's foreign policy posture plays into how other states respond to requests. Leveraging of crucial linkages is best done by those who are most well versed in all aspects of ties. However, inputs of ground realities too are important. Keeping faith in those who are in the trenches is as necessary as exercising the breadth of authority that is always available to those at the apex.

It is normal to be confronted with surprises on account of loss of support from least expected quarters. Consistent efforts at nurturing and broadening ties with an array of diverse states provides space and autonomy when more important partners turn away in pursuit of their specific interests. Engagements and alignments can be pursued with key partners even when paths are different.

In diplomacy, it is important to fight to the finish. There always is more time than one thinks there is. In an era when everything of the instant variety is the flavour of choice, patience and biding one's time to wait for the right opportunity is as important as the desire to bring rapid closure. Timing is as important as any other ingredient of success. Going through the numerous ups and downs of the election made us realize that while fighting the good fight is important, so is an understanding of the time to end it.

Finally, it drove home the need to expand our diplomatic footprint. In 2017, we did not have a presence in more than seventy UN member states. This fed into the subsequent announcement of opening more Indian missions in Africa to add greater weight to India's diplomatic footprint beyond familiar lands.[13] While we have made significant increases, we still do not have a presence in fifty UN member states.

At the permanent mission in New York, as was perhaps also the case in many other Indian diplomatic outposts, the outcome engendered a sense of confidence that reflected in the day-to-day work. It imbued a belief that Indian diplomacy is capable of reaching seemingly insurmountable goals. In New York, it catalysed the belief that projects that are not considered 'doable' should be undertaken. Tiding over crisis situations while working with diverse partners hones diplomatic skills. Building on the experiences of the ICJ election process, our young diplomats joined those with similar approaches to excise references to the 'Belt and Road' in intergovernmental documents at the UN,[14] persistently followed up with key partners to have Masood Azhar designated in the UN's list of terrorists,[15] pushed back against China's and Pakistan's combined efforts to get the Security Council to pronounce on the revocation of Article 370 of the Indian Constitution,[16] and have kept the winning habit in elections going.[17]

While we were privileged to be in the trenches on the frontline, many of our colleagues toiled in back rooms in different parts of the globe to ensure a successful outcome. There are many unsung heroes. Collectively, we exorcised the ghosts of the past. In many small ways the efforts reflected subterranean changes in style and substance that were the building blocks of a much more confident approach to thinking about and implementing foreign policy goals. In India, the resonance of the successful outcome went far beyond the diplomatic establishment. It fed into a growing belief that with the right focus and direction, and with necessary adjustments, seemingly difficult changes for the better could be made to happen.

India's ICJ election victory in 2017 remains sui generis, and a feat hard for anyone else to match. Three years after Judge Bhandari's victory in 2017, the next cycle of elections to the ICJ were held on 11 and 12 November 2020. Great power competition rather than cooperation was the flavour of the times. Signals of the global order being in flux were evident all around. Yet, the elections were over in a single round in the Security Council and in two rounds in the General Assembly. The outcome did not throw up any surprises. All incumbent judges who contested were re-elected. Despite three Africans being in the fray, only the incumbent was elected. The regional apple cart that Judge Bhandari's election had upset was not disturbed further.

The US and China differ on numerous issues, including on various aspects of international law. These divergences are constantly reflected at the UN. However, China's candidate, Judge Xue Hanquin, the only nominee from amongst the permanent members, entered the fray with the endorsement of all the permanent members. She contested as the non-national candidate of twenty-seven National Groups, including the US,[18] and was re-elected.[19] Where enduring diplomatic interests coincide, everything else is set aside.

Notes

Prologue: Starting Off on the Wrong Foot

1. Prior to India's Independence, at the 5th plenary meeting of the UN General Assembly on 12 January 1946, India was elected to the eighteen-member ECOSOC in the first ballot. India got forty-two votes, well above the required majority of thirty-four. UNGA 5th plenary meeting, 12 January 1946, A/PV.5, p. 90, https://undocs.org/en/A/PV.5 (Retrieved on 25 October 2020).
2. UNGA 92nd plenary meeting, 30 September 1947, A/PV.92, p. 316, https://undocs.org/en/A/PV.92 (Retrieved on 25 October 2020).
3. Ibid, p. 321.
4. UNGA 92nd plenary meeting, 30 September 1947, A/PV.92, p. 321, https://undocs.org/en/A/PV.92 (Retrieved on 25 October 2020).

5. UNGA 109th plenary meeting, 13 November 1947, A/PV.109, p. 749, https://undocs.org/en/A/PV.109 (Retrieved on 25 October 2020).
6. Security Council document S/2019/10/Add.49, 9 December 2019, p. 3, https://undocs.org/en/S/2019/10/Add.49 (Retrieved on 25 October 2020).
7. UNGA 153rd plenary meeting, 22 October 1948, A/PV.153, p. 372, https://undocs.org/en/A/PV.153 (Retrieved on 25 October 2020).
8. For the terms 1950-51, 1972-73, 1977-78, 1984-85, 1991-92, 2011-12 and 2021-22.
9. UNGA 1462nd plenary meeting, 11 November 1966, A/PV.1462, p. 1, https://undocs.org/en/A/PV.1462 (Retrieved on 25 October 2020).
10. UNGA 2387th plenary meeting, A/PV.2387, 23 October 1975, p. 614, https://undocs.org/en/A/PV.2387 (Retrieved on 25 October 2020).
11. UNGA 39th plenary meeting of the 51st session, 21 October 1996, A/51/PV.39, p. 2, https://undocs.org/en/A/51/PV.39 (Retrieved on 25 October 2020).
12. UNGA 350th plenary meeting, 6 December 1951, A/PV.350, pp. 209–10 https://undocs.org/en/A/PV.350 (Retrieved on 25 October 2020).
13. UNGA 2075th plenary meeting, 30 October 1972, A/PV.2075, pp. 1-2, https://undocs.org/en/A/PV.2075 (Retrieved on 25 October 2020).
14. UNGA 48th plenary meeting, 5 November 1981, A/36/PV.48, pp. 859–60 https://undocs.org/en/A/36/PV.48 (Retrieved on 25 October 2020).
15. Judge R.S. Pathak in 1989 for a term of less than two years to fill a vacancy on account of Judge Nagendra Singh's death, and Judge Dalveer Bhandari in 2012 for a term of less than six years when Judge Awn Shawkat Al-Khasawneh left.

1: It Began with a Whisper

1. CV, Judge Dalveer Bhandari, https://www.icj-cij.org/public/ files/members-of-the-court-biographies/bhandari_en.pdf (Retrieved on 8 August 2020).
2. CV, Judge Awn Shawkat Al-Khasawneh, https://legal.un.org/ avl/pdf/ls/Al-Khasawneh_bio.pdf (Retrieved on 11 August 2020).
3. See ICJ Press Release 2012/1, 20 January 2012, https://www. icj-cij.org/public/files/press-releases/1/16861.pdf (Retrieved on 17 October 2020).
4. For UN Press Release, 27 April 2012, on ICJ election results, see https://www.un.org/press/en/2012/ga11230.doc.htm (Retrieved on 8 August 2020).
5. International Law Commission, https://legal.un.org/ilc/ (Retrieved on 8 August 2020)
6. International Tribunal for the Law of the Sea, https://www. itlos.org/en/main/latest-news/ (Retrieved on 8 August 2020).
7. For an authoritative monograph, see Robert Kolb, *The International Court of Justice* (Oxford; Portland, Oregon: Hart Publishing, 2013), p. 1362.
8. International Law Commission, https://legal.un.org/ilc/texts/ instruments/english/statute/statute.pdf (Retrieved on 21 October 2020).
9. Dapo Akande, 'Patrick Robinson of Jamaica Elected to the ICJ', *EJIL: Talk! Blog of the European Journal of International Law*, 18 November 2014, https://www.ejiltalk.org/patrick-robinson-of-jamaica-elected-to-the-icj/ (Retrieved on 21 October 2020).
10. Aditya Roy and Anmolam, 'International Law: Sacrificing India's Reputation at the Altar of Petty Political Gain' *The Wire*, 7 November 2016, https://thewire.in/diplomacy/

decoding-indias-surprising-nomination-to-the-international-law-commission (Retrieved on 21 October 2020).

11. CV, Judge Antônio Augusto Cançado Trindade, https://www.icj-cij.org/public/files/members-of-the-court-biographies/cancado_en.pdf (Retrieved on 8 August 2020).

12. CV, Judge Ronny Abraham, https://www.icj-cij.org/public/files/members-of-the-court-biographies/abraham_en.pdf (Retrieved on 25 October 2020).

13. CV, Judge Abdulqawi Ahmed Yusuf, https://www.icj-cij.org/public/files/members-of-the-court-biographies/yusuf_en.pdf (Retrieved on 13 June 2021).

14. CV, Judge Christopher Greenwood, https://legal.un.org/avl/pdf/ls/Greenwood_bio.pdf (Retrieved on 8 August 2020).

15. Press Trust of India, 'India's Aniruddha Rajput Elected To UN's International Law Commission', *NDTV*, 4 November 2016, https://www.ndtv.com/india-news/indias-aniruddha-rajput-elected-to-uns-international-law-commission-1621289 (Retrieved on 8 August 2020).

16. See results of candidates from the Asia-Pacific group 2016, Election of the International Law Commission, https://legal.un.org/ilc/elections/2016election_outcome.shtml (Retrieved on 26 October 2020).

17. UNGA 350th plenary meeting, 6 December 1951, A/PV.350, pp. 209–10, https://undocs.org/en/A/PV.350 (Retrieved on 25 October 2020).

18. UNGA 2075th plenary meeting, 30 October 1972, A/PV.2075, p. 1, https://undocs.org/en/A/PV.2075 (Retrieved on 25 October 2020), and UNGA 48th plenary meeting of the 36th session, 5 November 1981, A/36/PV.48 ,p859-860, https://undocs.org/en/A/36/PV.48 (Retrieved on 25 October 2020).

19. UNGA 152nd plenary meeting, 22 October 1948, A/PV.152, pp. 368–70 https://undocs.org/A/PV.152 (Retrieved on

26 October 2020), and UNGA 153rd plenary meeting, 22 October 1948, A/PV.152, p. 371–72, https://undocs.org/A/PV.153 (Retrieved on 26 October 2020).

20. UNGA 1790th plenary meeting, 27 October 1969, A/PV.1790, p. 1, https://undocs.org/en/A/PV.1790 (Retrieved 26 October 2020).

21. UNGA 493rd plenary meeting, 7 October 1954, A/PV.493, p. 241, https://undocs.org/A/PV.493 (Retrieved 26 October 2020).

22. UNGA 91st plenary meeting of the 43rd session, 18 April 1989, A/43/PV.91, p. 11, https://undocs.org/en/A/43/PV.91 (Retrieved 26 October 2020).

23. UNGA 38th plenary meeting of the 45th session, 15 November 1990, A/45/PV.38, pp. 27–30, https://undocs.org/en/A/45/PV.38 (Retrieved 26 October 2020).

24. UNGA 107th plenary meeting of the 67th session, 27 April 2012, A/66/PV.107, p. 3, https://undocs.org/en/A/66/PV.107 (Retrieved 26 October 2020).

25. CV, Judge Awn Shawkat Al-Khasawneh, https://legal.un.org/avl/pdf/ls/Al-Khasawneh_bio.pdf (Retrieved on 11 August 2020).

26. For India's application to institute ICJ proceedings, see https://www.icj-cij.org/public/files/case-related/168/168-20170508-APP-01-00-EN.pdf (Retrieved on 8 August 2020).

27. Vienna Convention on Consular Relations, https://legal.un.org/ilc/texts/instruments/english/conventions/9_2_1963.pdf (Retrieved on 8 August 2020).

28. For ICJ Order on Provisional Measures, see https://icj-cij.org/files/case-related/168/168-20170518-ORD-01-00-EN.pdf (Retrieved on 8 August 2020).

29. See The Statute of the International Court of Justice, https://www.icj-cij.org/en/statute (Retrieved on 8 October 2020).

2: Come with a Plan, Not as a Plaintiff

1. See Results of 2016 Election of the International Law Commission, https://legal.un.org/ilc/elections/2016election_outcome.shtml (Retrieved on 26 October 2020).
2. See Akshaya Kumar, 'UN Human Rights Council Elections, Not Much of a Race After All: France Bows Out, Leaving an Open Field', *Human Rights Watch*, 14 July 2017, https://www.hrw.org/news/2017/07/14/un-human-rights-council-elections-not-much-race-after-all (Retrieved on 25 October 2020).
3. For details of the Shanghai Cooperation Organization, see http://eng.sectsco.org/ (Retrieved on 25 October 2020).

3: Big and Small—All Are in the Fray

1. Press Trust of India, 'Neeru Chadha becomes 1st Indian woman as member of ITLOS', *The Hindu*, 15 June 2017, https://www.thehindu.com/news/international/neeru-chadha-becomes-1st-indian-woman-as-member-of-itlos/article19053500.ece.
2. CV, Judge Chaloka Beyani, UN document A/72/183, https://undocs.org/A/72/183 (Retrieved on 18 August 2020).
3. In addition to the five permanent members—China, France, Russia, the UK and the US—the ten non-permanent members of the Security Council in 2017 were Bolivia, Egypt, Ethiopia, Italy, Japan, Kazakhstan, Senegal, Sweden, Ukraine and Uruguay.

4: Learning from History

1. See UNGA 72nd session, 20 July 2017, A/72/181–S/2017/619, p. 1, https://undocs.org/A/72/181 (Retrieved on 25 October

2020). Later, Sri Lanka's National Group also joined in support of Judge Bhandari.

2. See UNGA 72nd session, 12 November 2014, A/69/575, pp. 1–2, https://undocs.org/A/69/575 (Retrieved on 25 October 2020).

3. Withdrawal of Zambia candidate: UNGA 72nd session, 1 September 2017, A/72/182/Add.1–S/2017/620/Add.1, p. 1, https://undocs.org/A/72/182/Add.1 (Retrieved on 25 October 2020).

4. Statement by Shahid Khaqan Abbasi, Prime Minister of the Islamic Republic of Pakistan, at the General Debate of the 72nd session of the UN General Assembly on 21 September 2017, https://gadebate.un.org/sites/default/files/gastatements/72/pk_en.pdf (Retrieved on 25 October 2020).

5. Address by External Affairs Minister of the Republic of India, at the General Debate of the 72nd session of the UN General Assembly on 23 September 2017, https://gadebate.un.org/sites/default/files/gastatements/72/in_en.pdf (Retrieved on 25 October 2020).

6. India's Right of Reply, UNGA72, 21 September 2017, https://pminewyork.gov.in/pdf/uploadpdf/89670right%20of%20reply.pdf (Retrieved on 25 October 2020).

7. India's Right of Reply, UNGA72, 25 September 2017, https://www.pminewyork.gov.in/IndiaatUNGA?id=MzUxNg (Retrieved on 7 August 2021).

5: We Have Done Well, So Have the Others

1. IBSA Fund, http://www.ibsa-trilateral.org/ibsa_fund.html (Retrieved on 16 September 2020).

2. India–UN Development Partnership Fund, https://www.unsouthsouth.org/partner-with-us/india-un-fund/ (Retrieved on 16 September 2020).

3. 'Climate Early Warning Systems Project for Pacific Island States receives India-UN Development Partnership Fund support', *UNOSSC*, 16 June 2017, https://www.unsouthsouth.org/2017/06/16/climate-early-warning-systems-project-for-pacific-island-states-receives-india-un-development-partnership-fund-support/ (Retrieved on 16 September 2020).

4. Press Trust of India, 'India announces $200,000 emergency aid for hurricane-hit Caribbean countries', *Hindustan Times*, 20 September 2017, https://www.hindustantimes.com/india-news/india-announces-200-000-emergency-aid-for-hurricane-hit-caribbean-countries/story-FVDqrFU4BzmUTr2WHHqF7O.html (Retrieved on 16 September 2020).

5. The Fund at the end of 2020 had fifty projects drawing upon India's commitment of $150 million over a ten-year period.

6. See Edward McWhinney, 'Law, Politics and Regionalism in the Nomination and Election of World Court Judges,' *Syracuse Journal of International Law and Commerce* 13, No. 1 (Fall 1986): p. 15, https://heinonline.org/HOL/UNLAV?document_id=17700&ext=.pdf (Retrieved on 7 August 2021).

7. UNGA 493rd plenary meeting, 7 October 1954, A/PV.493, p. 241, https://undocs.org/A/PV.493 (Retrieved on 25 October 2020).

8. UNGA 71st session, 20 September 2017, A/RES/71/323, p. 8, https://undocs.org/en/a/res/71/323 (Retrieved on 16 September 2020).

6: What Is Happening?

1. UNGA 44th plenary meeting, 9 November 2017, A/72/PV44, p. 3–4, https://undocs.org/en/A/72/pv.44 (Retrieved on 25 October 2020).

2. UNGA 44th plenary meeting, 9 November 2017, A/72/PV44, p. 4, https://undocs.org/en/A/72/pv.44 (Retrieved on 25 October 2020).

7: A Contest by Chance, Not Choice

1. UNGA 44th plenary, 9 November 2017, A/72/PV.44, p. 5, https://undocs.org/en/A/72/pv.44 (Retrieved on 25 October 2020).
2. UNGA 45th plenary meeting, 9 November 2017, A/72/PV.45, p. 2, https://undocs.org/A/72/PV.45 and https://undocs.org/S/PV.8092%20(RESUMPTION%201) (Retrieved on 25 October 2020).
3. UNGA 53rd meeting of the 39th session, 7 November 1984, A/39/PV.53, p. 962, https://undocs.org/en/A/39/PV.53 (Retrieved on 27 October 2020).
4. AP, 'Peking judge chosen for World Court Section A,' *New York Times*, 8 November 1984, p. 9, https://www.nytimes.com/1984/11/08/world/around-the-world-peking-judge-chosen-for-world-court.html.
5. House of Commons Foreign Affairs Committee Report on the 2017 elections to the International Court of Justice, p. 8, https://publications.parliament.uk/pa/cm201719/cmselect/cmfaff/860/86004.htm (Retrieved on 21 October 2020).
6. UNGA 45th plenary meeting of the 72nd session, 9 November 2017, A/72/45 p. 2 https://digitallibrary.un.org/record/1466780, and the 8093rd meeting of the Security Council dated 9 November 2017, S/PV.8093, https://undocs.org/en/S/PV.8093 (Retrieved on 11 October 2020).
7. See S.D. Bailey and S. Daws, *The Procedure of the UN Security Council*, 3rd edition (Oxford: Clarendon Press, 1998), p. 312. cf. S. Rosenne, *The World Court: What It Is and How It Works*, 6th edition (Leiden: Brill-Nijhoff, 2003), p. 52.

8. See Press Release GA/10777, 6 November 2008, https://www.un.org/press/en/2008/ga10777.doc.htm (Retrieved on 21 October 2020).

8: I Punished Them the Only Way I Could

1. Memorandum by Professor Christopher Greenwood, CMG, QC, on 'The Legality of Using Force Against Iraq', UK Parliament Publications, https://publications.parliament.uk/pa/cm200203/cmselect/cmfaff/196/2102406.htm (Retrieved on 5 December 2020).
2. See 'Confluence of the Two Seas' Speech by Shinzo Abe, Prime Minister of Japan, at the Parliament of the Republic of India, 22 August 2007, https://www.mofa.go.jp/region/asia-paci/pmv0708/speech-2.html (Retrieved on 25 October 2020).
3. 'In 7 tweets, Shashi Tharoor slams UK over ICJ election; calls for reform at UN,' *India Today*, 14 November 2017, https://www.indiatoday.in/fyi/story/shashi-tharoor-icj-election-united-nations-general-assembly-uk-1085810-2017-11-14 (Retrieved on 25 October 2020).
4. See profile of Lord Ahmad of Wimbledon, https://www.gov.uk/government/people/lord-ahmad-of-wimbledon (Retrieved on 17 October 2020).
5. See profile of Christopher Weeramantry, 'For his lifetime of groundbreaking work to strengthen and expand the rule of international law,' *Right Livelihood*, https://www.rightlivelihoodaward.org/laureates/christopher-weeramantry/ (Retrieved on 17 October 2020).
6. In 2018 the members of the ICJ decided to end this practice and agreed that they will not normally participate in international arbitration. See p. 12 of speech by Judge Yusuf, then ICJ President, available at https://icj-cij.org/public/

files/press-releases/0/000-20181025-PRE-02-00-EN.pdf (Retrieved on 14 July 2021).

7.   Shortly thereafter, the Canadian International Institute of Sustainable Development put out a study that Greenwood was amongst the ICJ judges taking on several arbitration cases for which they are paid about $3,000 per day. Nathalie Bernasconi-Osterwalder and Martin Dietrich Brauch, 'Is "Moonlighting" a Problem? The role of ICJ judges in ISDS,' *International Institute of Sustainable Development* (November 2017), https://www.iisd.org/system/files/publications/icj-judges-isds-commentary.pdf (Retrieved on 10 December 2020).

8.   Impregilo SpA vs Islamic Republic of Pakistan, (ICSID) ARB/03/3, Decision of 22 April 2005; Bayindir Insaat Turizm Ticaret Ve Sanayi AS vs Islamic Republic of Pakistan, (ICSID) ARB/03/29, Decision of 14 November 2005; and Award of 27 April 2009, in which hearings concluded in 2008 before Greenwood joined the ICJ on 6 February 2009.

9: Let Us Leave It

1.   See Vijay Gokhale, 'Sushma Swaraj made MEA relevant to Indians,' *India Today*, 5 August 2020, https://www.indiatoday. in/india-today-insight/story/-sushma-swaraj-made-mea-relevant-to-indians-1708157-2020-08-05 (Retrieved on 17 October 2020).

2.   See the American Society of Law's International Law in Brief, 6 January 2012, https://web.archive.org/web/20120117155009/http://www.asil.org/ilib120106.cfm#j3. (Retrieved on 17 October 2020). See Statute of the ICJ on the website of the ICJ, https://www.icj-cij.org/en/statute (Retrieved on 12 October 2020).

3. See M.O. Hudson, 'The Permanent Court of International Justice,' *Harvard Law Review*, 35, No. 3 (January 1922): p. 250, https://www.jstor.org/stable/pdf/1329614.pdf (Retrieved on 12 October 2020).

4. Extracts from the UN Juridical Year Book 1984, p. 175: https://legal.un.org/unjuridicalyearbook/pdfs/english/by_volume/1984/chpVI.pdf (Retrieved on 12 October 2020).

5. See Statute of the ICJ on the website of the ICJ: https://www.icj-cij.org/en/statute (Retrieved on 15 October 2020).

6. See Sachin Parasher, 'UK resorting to Robert Clive tactics at UN to deny India ICJ,' *Times of India*, 19 November 2017, https://timesofindia.indiatimes.com/india/uk-threatens-to-invoke-unprecedented-mechanism-to-deny-india-icj-seat/articleshow/61706985.cms (Retrieved on 12 October 2020).

7. UNGA 2387th plenary meeting, 23 October 1975, A/PV.2387, pp. 611–15, https://undocs.org/A/PV.2387 (Retrieved on 18 October 2020).

8. UNGA 39th plenary meeting, 21 October 1996, A/51/PV.39, pp. 1–4, https://undocs.org/A/51/PV.39 (Retrieved on 18 October 2020).

10: Please Don't Pick Up the Phone

1. Extracts from the UN Juridical Year Book 1984, p. 175, https://legal.un.org/unjuridicalyearbook/pdfs/english/by_volume/1984/chpVI.pdf (Retrieved on 12 October 2020).

2. Robert Kolb, *The International Court of Justice* (Oxford; Portland, Oregon: Hart Publishing: 2013), p. 141.

3. UN Security Council 2093rd meeting, 31 October 1978, S/PV.2093, p. 1, https://undocs.org/en/S/PV.2093(OR).

4. UNGA 53rd plenary meeting of the 66th session, 10 November 2011, A/66/PV.53, pp. 1–3, https://undocs.org/en/A/66/PV.53 (Retrieved on 14 July 2021); UNGA 54th

plenary meeting of the 66th session, 10 November 2011, A/66/PV.54, pp. 1–3, https://undocs.org/en/A/66/PV.54 (Retrieved on 14 July 2021); UNGA 55th plenary meeting of the 66th session, 10 November 2011, A/66/PV.55, p. 1, https://undocs.org/en/A/66/PV.55 (Retrieved on 14 July 2021); UNGA 56th plenary meeting of the 66th session, 10 November 2011, A/66/PV.56, p. 1, https://undocs.org/en/A/66/PV.56 (Retrieved on 14 July 2021); and UNGA 57th plenary meeting of the 66th session, 10 November 2011, A/66/PV.57, p. 1, https://undocs.org/en/A/66/PV.57 (Retrieved on 14 July 2021).

Also see UNGA 64th plenary meeting of the 66th session, 22 November 2011, A/66/PV.64, pp. 1–3, https://undocs.org/en/A/66/PV.64 (Retrieved on 14 July 2021); UNGA 65th plenary meeting of the 66th session, 22 November 2011, A/66/PV.65, p. 1, https://undocs.org/en/A/66/PV.65 (Retrieved on 14 July 2021); and 66th plenary meeting of the 66th session, 22 November 2011, A/66/PV.66, p. 1, https://undocs.org/en/A/66/PV.66 (Retrieved on 14 July 2021).

Finally, UNGA 84th plenary meeting of the 66th session, 13 December 2011, A/66/PV.84, p. 1, https://undocs.org/en/A/66/PV.84 (Retrieved on 14 July 2021).

5. UNGA 39th plenary meeting of the 69th session, 6 November 2014, A/69/PV.39, pp. 1–7, https://undocs.org/en/A/69/PV.39 (Retrieved on 14 July 2021).

UNGA 40th–46th plenary meetings of the 69th session, 7 November 2014, A/69/PV.40–A/69/PV.46, https://undocs.org/en/A/69/PV.40; https://undocs.org/en/A/69/PV.41; https://undocs.org/en/A/69/PV.42; https://undocs.org/en/A/69/PV.43; https://undocs.org/en/A/69/PV.44; https://undocs.org/en/A/69/PV.45; and https://undocs.org/en/A/69/PV.46. Also see UNGA 53rd meeting of 69th session, 17 November 2014, A/69/PV.53 https://undocs.org/en/A/69/PV.53.

6. House of Commons Foreign Affairs Committee Report on the 2017 elections to the International Court of Justice, p. 7, https://publications.parliament.uk/pa/cm201719/cmselect/cmfaff/860/86004.htm (Retrieved on 15 October 2020).

Epilogue: Where Interests Coincide, Everything Is Kept Aside

1. Oliver Wright, 'Britain loses its seat at UN court for first time,' *The Times*, 21 November 2017, https://www.thetimes.co.uk/article/britain-loses-its-seat-at-un-court-for-first-time-8nm2cj7md (Retrieved on 7 August 2021).

2. Owen Bowcott, 'No British judge on world court for first time in its 71-year history,' *The Guardian*, 20 November 2017, https://www.theguardian.com/law/2017/nov/20/no-british-judge-on-world-court-for-first-time-in-its-71-year-history (Retrieved on 7 August 2021).

3. James Landale, 'How UK lost International Court of Justice place to India,' *BBC News*, 21 November 2017, https://www.bbc.com/news/uk-politics-42063664 (Retrieved on 21 October 2020).

4. House of Commons Foreign Affairs Committee Report on the 2017 elections to the International Court of Justice, p. 8, https://publications.parliament.uk/pa/cm201719/cmselect/cmfaff/860/86004.htm (Retrieved on 21 October 2020).

5. Vijay Gokhale, 'Sushma Swaraj made MEA relevant to Indians,' *India Today*, 5 August 2020, https://www.indiatoday.in/india-today-insight/story/-sushma-swaraj-made-mea-relevant-to-indians-1708157-2020-08-05 (Retrieved on 7 August 2021).

6. Varghese K. George, 'India pulls off a diplomatic coup, wins prized ICJ seat,' *The Hindu*, 21 November 2017, https://

www.thehindu.com/news/international/faced-with-defeat-uk-withdraws-india-wins-international-court-of-justice-seat/article20609566.ece (Retrieved on 7 August 2021).

7. Editorial, 'Turning Point,' *The Statesman*, 23 November 2017, https://www.thestatesman.com/opinion/turning-point-1502533233.html (Retrieved on 7 August 2021).

8. Press Trust of India, 'Modi praises Swaraj, Shah says "diplomatic win",' *Hindustan Times*, 21 November 2017, https://www.hindustantimes.com/india-news/pm-modi-credits-swaraj-for-re-election-of-india-s-bhandari-to-icj/story-DkHbSprump1fXQWO2310BL.html.

9. Harsh V. Pant, 'Power Shift: India's Nominee Re-Elected to ICJ,' *The Diplomat*, 21 December 2020, https://thediplomat.com/2017/11/power-shift-indias-nominee-re-elected-to-icj/ (Retrieved on 7 August 2021).

10. Bruno Gelinas Faucher, 'Election Season at the ICJ: Dawn of a New Era?' *Opiniojuris*, 29 July 2020, http://opiniojuris.org/2020/07/29/election-season-at-the-icj-dawn-of-a-new-era/ (Retrieved on 7 August 2021).

11. Arun Sukumar, 'The Significance of Dalveer Bhandari's, and India's, Recent Election to the ICJ,' *Lawfare*, 13 December 2017, https://www.lawfareblog.com/significance-dalveer-bhandaris-and-indias-recent-election-icj (Retrieved on 7 August 2021).

12. ICJ Press Release No. 2019/31, 17 July 2019 on Jadhav case (India vs Pakistan), https://www.icj-cij.org/public/files/case-related/168/168-20190717-PRE-01-00-EN.pdf (Retrieved on 28 October 2020).

13. Press Trust of India, 'Government to set up 18 new missions in Africa by 2021,' *Times of India*, 21 March 2018, https://timesofindia.indiatimes.com/india/government-to-set-up-18-new-missions-in-africa-by-2021/articleshow/63402998.cms (Retrieved on 7 August 2021).

14. Seema Sirohi, 'China Faces Pushback in the UN on Belt-Road Initiative, Retreats Quietly,' *The Wire*, 17 October 2017, https://thewire.in/diplomacy/china-obor-belt-road-un-pushback (Retrieved on 7 August 2021).

15. Sriram Lakshman and Suhasini Haider, 'UN designates JeM chief Masood Azhar as global terrorist,' *The Hindu*, 1 May 2019, https://www.thehindu.com/news/international/un-designates-jem-chief-masood-azhar-as-global-terrorist/article27002685.ece (Retrieved on 7 August 2021).

16. Elizabeth Roche, 'At UNSC, China and Pakistan fail to censure India over Article 370,' *The Mint*, 17 October 2020, https://www.livemint.com/news/india/at-unsc-china-and-pakistan-fail-to-censure-india-over-article-370-1565978919225.html (Retrieved on 7 August 2021).

17. Press Trust of India, 'India wins election to UNHRC with highest votes,' *Times of India*, 13 October 2018, https://timesofindia.indiatimes.com/india/india-wins-election-to-un-human-rights-council/articleshow/66186030.cms (Retrieved on 7 August 2021).

18. UN document dated 29 January 2020, A/75/129-S/2020/615, p. 6, https://undocs.org/A/75/129 (Retrieved on 13 July 2021).

19. UN Security Council Press Release SC/14357 of 12 November 2020, https://www.un.org/press/en/2020/sc14357.doc.htm (Retrieved on 13 July 2021).

Index

INDEX

Acknowledgements

SOME ASCRIBE IT to chance; others describe it as luck. Some term it as good fortune; and the believers often attribute it to God's grace. Call it what you may, the rare opportunity to be part of the meritocracy drawn from so many who aspire to serve India also opens up doors that one cannot envisage when the journey begins. I am indebted to the Indian system of providing meritocratic public service career platforms that enabled me to pursue my passion for international relations as a life-long career in diplomacy.

Observing and analysing events and communicating them in a comprehensible way comes as second nature to diplomats. Transitioning to a new phase, following decades of peripatetic existence as a modern-day nomad, doesn't end that perennial quest to join the dots, make sense of change and explain it. However, without Siddhesh Inamdar of HarperCollins approaching me and expressing willingness to publish any aspect of my experiences that I was willing to share with a wider audience, I wouldn't have written this book. To him and his establishment, I am grateful for navigating this venture from incubation to completion.

But for the willing support of numerous former colleagues of the Indian Foreign Service and fellow diplomats from several other countries, I couldn't have recalled the events of this narrative in such detail. The final manuscript owes much to the long hours put in by Lakshmi and Swaminathan, who had worked with me in New York, and did much of the research of the official UN records and review and correction of the initial drafts of the manuscript, despite their other preoccupations.

Diplomatic families tend to become tight-knit units and also the first ports of call whenever advice and constructive criticism are needed. Without a catalyst in the form of my wife, Padma, and the distant yet constant oversight of my sons, Sai and Samir, I would have been happy honing my golfing skills rather than writing of this experience at the United Nations.

This effort is dedicated to all members of India's growing diplomatic fraternity. While I owe much to the many who have helped me in numerous ways, I accept the entire responsibility for errors or oversights, if any.

About the Author

Syed Akbaruddin has been amongst the most visible faces of Indian diplomacy in recent times. In a diplomatic career spanning thirty-five years, he spent more than a decade engaged in multilateral diplomacy—both as an Indian diplomat and an international civil servant. He served as India's Permanent Representative to the UN from 2016 till his retirement from the Indian Foreign Service in 2020. Now the Dean of the Kautilya School of Public Policy, he lives in Hyderabad with his wife, Padma Akbaruddin.